GLASGOW'S HARD MEN

GLASGOW'S HARD MEN

TRUE CRIME FROM THE FILES OF THE HERALD,
EVENING TIMES AND SUNDAY HERALD

ROBERT JEFFREY

BLACK & WHITE PUBLISHING

First published 2002
This edition
first published 2006
by Black & White Publishing Ltd
99 Giles Street, Edinburgh EH6 6BZ

ISBN 13: 978 1 84502 132 0
ISBN 10: 1 84502 132 0

A CIP catalogue record for this book
is available from The British Library.

Photographs courtesy of SMG Newspapers Limited

Printed and bound by Nørhaven Paperback A/S

CONTENTS

ACKNOWLEDGEMENTS

This book could not have been written without the work of countless *Herald*-group journalists down the years. Dedicated feature writers, big-name columnists, photographers and hard working anonymous rota reporters have produced one of the world's great archives. They conducted the interviews, reported the murders, arrests and court cases down the years. Every facet of life in Glasgow and its surrounds over the last 200 years has been faithfully chronicled. From these files have been culled some of the great stories of the battle against crime in the city.

I would also like to acknowledge the assistance of Marie Jeffrey, Samantha Boyd, Jackie Borrett, Kingsley Borrett, Ian Watson, John Watson and the staff of the SMG Publishing Division library: Stroma Fraser, Pip Ryan, Jim McNeish, Maris Thomson, Kathleen Smith, Natalie Bushe, Angela Laurins, Malcolm Beaton, Sara Stewart, Tony Murray, Eva Mutter, Catherine Turner, Lisa Turner and Grace Gough.

INTRODUCTION

Travelling abroad around 30 years ago, in the heyday of the package holiday, many a Glaswegian habitually disguised their roots. Where are you from? That was a standard hotel bar opener as the first Cuba Libres slipped speedily over throats parched by the Majorcan sun and with the annual fortnight's escape from the tyranny of shipyard or steelworks stretching thirstily ahead. Holidaymakers from Govan, Garthamlock or Garngad tended to mumble a reply about the West of Scotland, or Lanarkshire or whatever. Anything for an easy life. To admit upfront to the Sassenach hordes that you were a gold-plated Glaswegian could provoke an ill-informed suspicion that you had left an open razor handy in the bedroom drawer, or that your days in the sun had been financed by unauthorised withdrawals from the handbags of dear old ladies.

Such was the worldwide misconception about Glasgow in the days when the image of *No Mean City* – Alexander McArthur's controversial and often misunderstood novel depicting the pre-Second World War gangs and gangsters – ruled and the Glasgow Smiles Better campaign, the Garden Festival and European City of Culture were distant dreams. It is hard now in the dawning days of the 21st century to realise how potent that image was to folk who had never crossed Glasgow's city boundary.

It was a different story for those who grew up in a place that was often unfairly called the Chicago of Europe, or accused of making Marseilles look like a garden suburb. Knowledge of the city's deep-rooted image in the collective consciousness of most of the world was hard to avoid. Sometimes it was simply the menacing strut of some young gang member seen fleetingly in the street. Or it could be much worse.

As a youngster growing up in the sheltered streets of Croftfoot – a south-side suburb of tidy, rented, four-in-a-block houses with gardens in front and a normally well-kept drying-green at the back – big-time crime was not normally overly visible, even if the local ironmonger did a good trade in chains and padlocks for bicycles. Croftfoot and Kings Park, its slightly more upmarket neighbour, had their own leafy park and even a nice little nine-hole golf course set on a steep hillside – a course that had been memorably described in a series of newspaper articles by the famous amateur golfer turned sportswriter, Eddie Hamilton, as a place where the biggest advantage one golfer could have over another was to have one leg shorter than the other.

It was to such wide open places that youngsters from less prosperous areas like nearby Bridgeton tended to roam looking for trouble with the suburban kids. One day my school pals and I found ourselves in a minor rumble with a group of Brigton boys who told us proudly that they were members of a gang called the Biro Minors. This undeniably witty title reflected the fact that they thought their peers were the infamous Bridgeton Pen Gang, the original Biro Minor being the then innovative ball-point pen. The Croftfoot boys were suitably and speedily impressed and fled to their mums, an early introduction to the continuing heritage of *No Mean City*.

Childhood visits to an aunt originally from Armagh, a place that is no stranger to violence, brought other tales of Bridgeton in the days before the legendary Chief Constable Percy Sillitoe – 'The Captain' to his men – took on the gangs and helped to begin the slow claw-back from the image of the razor slashers and gangland warfare that, no matter how often it is denied or described as exaggerated, stuck to Glasgow for too many years.

Starting work as a journalist in the 1950s, Glasgow's image of a tough place to live and work was further defined. The papers themselves relied heavily on crime to sell. At the top end of the scale there were undignified scrums outside the High Court as rival hacks fought to buy up the stories of participants in major trials. Criminals who had never ventured more than a couple of miles away from a spit-and-sawdust howff and the booze-swilling company of their foul-mouthed mates were whisked to four-star hotels to spill the inside story of their misdemeanours over a bottle of malt. With a nice cheque served with breakfast the next morning.

The most memorable of these street battles was the occasion when famous Glasgow underworld figure Walter Scott Ellis was freed on a charge of murdering a taxi driver. He was said to have been bought up by one of the city's morning newspapers, but was bundled into an *Evening Citizen* car in a skirmish. At the height of this mini-riot it was said that a man with a broken leg was flaying out at all and sundry with his crutch. This event, notorious in newspaper history, led to a judgement by Lord Clyde on how cases in Scotland should in future be handled by the Press. Although modified over the years, the strictures imposed by this case still affect how newspapers deal with police investigations to this day. And of course, these days the Press Complaints Commission has a strict policy on not allowing criminals to benefit financially from their crimes – though this self-regulation has its critics and there is on-going argument about the definition of financial benefit.

At the other end of the crime-scale, stair-heid rammies and minor feuds were reported in great detail. These were the days of hot-metal journalism with the popular papers heavily staffed with crime reporters, a breed who spent their proprietors' cash with abandon building up the allegedly vital contacts book. The old joke was that some of the best had such good sources for tip-offs and contacts that they could not write about them for fear of exposing the source! The stories they did get into print were sub-edited by veterans, often ex-reporters who had come off the road to settle for a warm desk and the comfort of a bottle of Scotch in the bottom drawer as they crafted the eye-catching intro and headline required by editors with an eye on circulation. One of my first jobs was on the now defunct *Bulletin,* and on my first night in the then Buchanan Street printing plant one such wise old sub-editor asked me where I stayed and how I planned to get home. He gave me a gem of advice for my early morning stroll back to the southside . . . always walk down the middle of the street as this gives you 10 or 12 yards' start on assailants emerging from close-mouths.

But even in this sort of Glasgow it was, as always, a war with two sides. The newspapers who so carefully chronicled the gangs, the robbers and the drug barons also had a cast of heroes. Particularly the cops. The city needed tough Chief Constables and they had a succession of them from Sillitoe to Robertson to McNee and many others – men who wrote themselves into the city's history as hard as anyone on the other side of the crime divide. The PC on the beat in Glasgow has always had an unenviable job, but at least they have the satisfaction of being led by Big Men. A cynic might remark that the exploits of the police created as much interest and sold as many papers as the crimes of the gangs . . . The Billy Boys, the Norman Conks, the Baltic Fleet and all the rest of the villains.

And the lawyers – characters like the great pleaders Lawrence Dowdall, Joe Beltrami and Donald Findlay – and sheriffs and judges grabbed headlines too, from Irvine Smith to Lord Carmont and many more. But they did more than just fill the crime pages of newspapers; they dispensed justice and helped turn the tide in a city's remarkable fight against crime. Often, these great characters made as firm an impression on the public mind as the criminals.

The many tales in the pages of this book, drawn from the irreplaceable archive of *The Herald, Evening Times* and *Sunday Herald,* are a tribute to the dedicated reporters and feature writers who worked for Scotland's greatest newspaper down the years. To completely cover the tales of Glasgow's crime in the huge files would take volumes – but this is a selection of the fascinating doings of the good guys and the bad guys of one of Europe's great cities. A city with a past. But whose people now, when asked where they are from, would not fail to reply with pride – 'Glasgow'. Some things do change.

1

A DOCTOR, A LADY
AND A HANGMAN

In the heady days of Glasgow's newspaper circulation battles – in the '50s and '60s when the crime reporter was king, and the papers recorded every late-night mugging or minor gang feud with much the same intensity they awarded High Court trials – the *Express* group was billeted in Albion Street, eventually to become home to the *Herald* from the '70s till the new millennium.

The thirsty hacks of those distant days felt that time spent in the office was time wasted. Their natural home was the pub. And in Albion Street the main beneficiaries of this way of life were the McEntee family who ran the Press Bar, in reality always known as 'Tom's' in honour of the founder who was followed into the business by his three sons, Leo, Gerry and Desi. But sometimes there was business to be done away from the nearest bar to the office. And for many a reporter that meant a temporary transfer of thirst-busting to a rather grimy little establishment just off Candleriggs called 'The Hangman's Rest'. One of the *Express's* bright young men, obviously bound for Fleet Street, took a quick blink at the chrome and Formica of a pub on its descent into memory and suggested that a more appropriate name might be 'The Electric Chair'. Nonetheless this sad place was a macabre reminder of the days when the gallows were a feature of the nearby Saltmarket.

Hanging was no novelty in Glasgow. It is said that the first hangings took place in what was known as Hangman's Brae, which became part of Ladywell Street in the Drygate. However, most of the executions from 1814 to 1865 attracted the crowds to Saltmarket. During these years the scaffold faced east towards Nelson's monument in Glasgow Green. All this meant a double, if deadly, distinction for the infamous surgeon Dr Edward Pritchard. More than 80,000 people turned out to see him meet his maker – thus becoming both the last man to be publicly executed in Glasgow and the last man to die on the gallows in the time-honoured Glasgow phrase, 'facing the monument'.

The Pritchard tale would have been meat and drink to the modern tabloids and would no doubt have spawned a TV mini-series – if not a full-scale Hollywood treatment. The doctor's wife had died, and at the funeral some reports have it that Pritchard kissed the corpse with tears in his eyes – a show of emotion that temporarily allowed him to play the grieving compassionate husband. In fact, he had been slowly poisoning both his wife and his mother-in-law and suspicion only fell on him when an anonymous letter was sent to the Procurator Fiscal. It didn't take the Inspector Morses of the day long to find chemists who could confirm that the doctor had been building up supplies of poisons in quantities suspicious even for a medical man. The speculation was that financial problems or an affair with a former servant lay behind the crime, a deed so horrific that it caught the public imagination to the extent that 80,000 travelled to the Green to watch the hangman perform his grisly task. It seemed fitting somehow that many years later, workmen digging the foundations for the city mortuary in Jocelyn Square in the Saltmarket found the skeleton of the legendary wife-beater and poisoner who lived in Sauchiehall Street.

Around 1875, Duke Street Prison, close by the Cathedral, became the official place for executions which were now carried out in private. Later the gallows moved to Barlinnie where on 8 February 1946 a 21-year-old called John Lyon was hanged for his part in the murder of a Royal Navy sailor in Washington Street. It was the first hanging in the city since George Reynolds, who had killed a bakehouse worker, was hanged in Duke Street. By the time young Lyon had met his fate the macabre practice of flying a black flag over the prison to mark the execution had been dropped.

Even in the early days, when the gallows were such a feature of criminal life, not every killer ended up dancing on the end of a rope. The ability of a good lawyer could turn a case, for or against. Two classic examples are to be found in the *Herald* files. In their differing ways the Madeleine Smith case and that of Oscar Slater are forever entwined in the city's history of crime. Madeleine Smith's escape from the charge of murdering her French lover Pierre Emile L'Angelier with a cup of cocoa laced with arsenic (poison seemed something of a city speciality in these days) was perhaps the most famous 'not proven' case in the history of that controversial verdict. The fitting-up of the seedy loser Oscar Slater for a murder he did not commit also became a legendary crime story. Both cases sparked a raft of books, and in Madeleine's case a film and several plays.

It is easy to see why the Smith case attracted such attention. Most contemporary reports describe her as 'plumpish', then considered no disadvantage in a young woman, since this was long before the days of heroin-chic or waif-like models earning millions a year. Madeleine seems to have possessed a certain passionate air which certainly captivated young L'Angelier, a Channel Islander of French extraction who worked for a small wage in a seedsman's office in Bothwell Street. Pierre was, according to reports, a bit of a dandy. At her trial in Edinburgh's High Court in March 1857, an astonishing tale of passion, poison and deception emerged – holding the attention of the nation for the nine days that it lasted.

For a 22-year-old in such a dramatic situation Madeleine's self-possession seems to have been remarkable. The legendary Glasgow journalist Jack House, who chronicled the Smith story in his book

Square Mile of Murder, was impressed with contemporary reports in the London Press that 'her head never sank for a moment, and she even seemed to scan the witnesses with a scrutinising glance. Her perfect self-possession indeed could only be accounted for either by a proud consciousness of innocence, or by her possessing an almost unparalleled amount of self-control. She even smiled with all the airs and graces of a young lady in the drawing-room as her agents came forward to communicate with her.' That it was self-control rather than innocence is perhaps evidenced by the fact that in later life in America she is alleged to have admitted the crime. Though, all these years later, there is still support for the theory that L'Angelier supplied the arsenic and plotted to make her seem guilty. Her lawyer John Inglis is thought by some to have been a brilliant pleader who won her freedom. Indeed, it was top-class defence work costing £8000 – half a million in today's money – but not everyone gives him all the credit. As recently as 1997, Ted Ramsay wrote a letter to the *Herald* crediting the jury for the verdict, rather than Inglis' closing speech. This theory has it that the prosecution relied heavily on a witness called James Towers, who told the court about L'Angelier boasting that Madeleine had twice tried to poison him with arsenic.

The fact is that something dramatic must have happened in the jury room for all the evidence that had gone before to be disregarded, and it took a mere 25 minutes to declare the case against Madeleine not proven. There is a belief that someone in the jury recognised Towers as an unreliable figure and convinced other jurors that a prosecution founded on such shaky ground in this issue didn't deserve a guilty verdict. But the story of the wealthy architect's daughter and her humble and unsuitable suitor has a remarkable longevity. At the time of the crime Madeleine was thought to be a bit of a tease, and her letters about her intimacy with the Channel Islander were extremely direct for the era, causing some scandal when read out in the court. Examined now, the evidence put before the court was indeed very convincing of her guilt; but Towers apart, the jury did hear some interesting material that pointed to her innocence. For instance one medical expert stated that the amount of arsenic found in the victim's stomach was far beyond what one person could administer to another. It seems that there was a clear majority of the jury for the not-proven verdict, based on cautions from the bench about the need for absolute certainty when dealing with such a crime. But the Press afterwards reported that most jurors actually believed she was guilty. You can't help feeling that her 'respectability' and that of her family swayed the jurors – and that as in the Slater case, people believed that those of a certain class could not be murderers.

Madeleine went south to London and in 1861 married an artist called George J Wardle. Her self-possession remained intact, and by all accounts her conscience about the disposal of a lover who had become a nuisance to herself and to her society family did not bother her. Indeed, she settled in Bloomsbury with George – who also did not seem concerned about the stories of her past – and became part of Socialist society. An intriguing part of her story is that as a hostess she invented the style of doing away with tablecloths on swanky dinner tables, replacing them with individual mats. She moved in London political society, mingling with the likes of George Bernard Shaw, Sidney Webb and Karl Marx's son-in-law Edward Aveling. Around 1916 she moved to America where her son Tom lived and she died in the Bronx in 1928 at the age of 92. Some years before her death, according to Somerset Maugham, she admitted that she had killed Pierre and that if in the same circumstances she would do it again. Self-possessed to the end.

The turn of the century brought another case that has filled the columns of the *Herald* and fuelled controversy over the years – the conviction, near-hanging and unjust incarceration of Oscar Slater. This was a case lacking in the spicy sexual overtones of the Smith case, but it had yet another dimension and didn't really end until almost 100 years after the killing. A few days before Christmas 1908 a rich 83-year-old spinster called Marion Gilchrist, living in fashionable West Princes Street, was battered to death by a mystery assailant. The old lady had earlier sent her maid out for a paper and when the servant returned she found a neighbour at the door. He said he had been alerted by a loud thud minutes before. Suddenly a well-dressed stranger brushed past them, making for the head of the stairs, and then took to his heels. The maid and the neighbour went into the dining room where they found the injured Miss Gilchrist. A short while later she was dead. The only thing missing seemed to be a gold and diamond brooch.

From this simple scenario the remarkable story of the fitting-up of Oscar Slater began. Slater had some sort of 'form', though nothing that would make him a murder suspect. The police were under enormous pressure to find the person behind this shocking crime and the name Oscar Slater cropped up when a tip-off claimed that he had tried to sell a pawn ticket for a brooch. Slater was a German Jew with a sleazy reputation: he lived with a showbiz mistress and was a gambler and jewel dealer. Investigation soon proved that the jewellery sold by Slater was not the brooch taken from old Miss Gilchrist. But Oscar and his paramour had gone at short notice to New York, travelling under assumed names, and the police believed that he had fled because of newspaper reports that seemed to say he resembled the man seen at the scene of the crime. The shameful fit-up had started. Slater was arrested in New York and returned of his own free will to face trial, no doubt confident that no police force in the world could link him to this crime in which he had no involvement. This was misplaced optimism that almost cost him his life.

An identification parade was rigged with witnesses prompted to finger poor Oscar. His trial provided virtually no solid evidence against him other than dodgy identification and hatred in the city for a foreigner who had been convicted by public opinion. The actual trial verged on the farcical. Slater was condemned to death but rather mysteriously reprieved a couple of days before the execution. He went on to serve 18 years before being freed after much campaigning involving amongst others, Sir Arthur Conan Doyle. The story had a great grip on public opinion and down the years the *Herald* covered the twists and turns of one of the world's greatest tales of injustice. One of the strongest theories involved members of Miss Gilchrist's family who were exceedingly well connected – another theory involves the maid, Helen Lambie, said to be secretly engaged to one of the suspects. Yet another postulates that the killer or killers were straightforward Glasgow thieves who targeted the old lady's jewel hoard.

The truth will probably never be known, but the fact that Slater was framed is in no doubt and there is evidence of reports about him being doctored. One unique aspect of the case is the story of Detective John Trench of the Glasgow Police Force, who has had *Herald* stories written about him for almost 100 years. In the early '90s evidence emerged to show that the detective was a man of integrity who had attempted to expose how the police and senior legal figures had conspired to lie at the trial. All this was a bit on the late side for the honest cop, for five years after Slater was jailed and still with another 13 to go till freedom, Trench had tried to pass information to the Secretary of State that the wrong man was banged up in Peterhead doing hard labour. Lieutenant Trench had given information to a Glasgow solicitor on why he believed Slater was innocent. A sham inquiry was set up and Trench's research dismissed – and as a thank-you for his efforts, the honest cop was dismissed from the force for passing information to an outsider!

In yet another astonishing twist in this rotten case, when Slater was finally freed in 1928 Trench was not officially rehabilitated. The detective had served in the army during the First World War but had died in a 1919 flu epidemic. Indeed, to the very end the Slater/Trench affair had curiously unsatisfactory overtones. Slater was never declared not guilty; his conviction was quashed on a technicality. But he lived quietly until 1948 making many friends and leading a respectable life. As for Trench, in 1998 Scottish

Secretary Donald Dewar found no statutory authority to issue a pardon or posthumous rehabilitation. A review by the Scottish Office found Trench had acted with 'moral conviction'. Mr Dewar found Trench's dismissal was harsh but there was no power to intervene. According to the politicians Trench should have challenged his 1914 dismissal in a court of law. Authority seemed to have had the last word in a memorable case where an innocent man barely escaped the hangman and a fighter for justice found his reputation besmirched. But in a gesture of reconciliation, in 1999 Strathclyde Chief Constable John Orr invited Trench's daughter – 87-year-old Nancy Stark – to a ceremony to mark his memory and arranged a commemorative panel to go on display at the force museum in Pitt Street.

2

DEATH IN THE BAR-L

For most Glaswegians, Barlinnie Prison is a grim fortress glimpsed from a speeding car on the M8. Even such a fleeting acquaintance with Glasgow's legendary place of incarceration and execution can set the imagination racing. Stand outside the wall and the grimness of this Victorian building seeps into your soul. Inside, the visitor is overwhelmed by the noise, smell and the sight of men held in appalling conditions. During the 19th century Glasgow had no fewer than eight prisons, but by 1840 only two were left: Burgh at Glasgow Green which closed in 1862, and Duke Street, which closed in 1955. Completed in 1894, Barlinnie was built on East End farmland and was designed to alleviate overcrowding in the existing jails. It was built to hold 1000 prisoners in four five-storey blocks, making it the largest prison in Scotland. Ironically, to this day it still contains on occasion the same number of inmates. Not much has changed down the years.

In the early months of 2000 Scotland's Chief Inspector of Prisons, Clive Fairweather, criticised cells containing chamber-pots in a 'filthy, encrusted state' and mattresses and beds that were possible fire hazards. His damning report also highlighted chronic overcrowding. The prisoners facing the worst conditions were on remand, untried and unconvicted. And at the end of the 20th century the degrading practice of slopping-out – the emptying of chamber-pots by the prisoners – was still a disgusting ritual. In some areas of the Bar-L little has changed in 100 years. But in other areas of the prison there have been big improvements in the way in which prisoners are held, particularly in the High Dependency Unit where since the mid-'90s money has been spent. But much of the trouble with Barlinnie is simply its age and design. To convert it into a modern prison will take many years and many millions. Even when that happens – if it ever does – nothing can erase the grim memories of this place. Strangely for such a violent city, there was a gap of 17 years – from 1929 to 1946 – between the last hanging in the old Duke Street Prison and the first in Barlinnie. The infamous distinction of being the first man to lose his life in the Hanging Shed was a young man called John Lyon. Only 21, he paid with his life for his part in the murder of John Brady, a Navy man, in Washington Street.

There was no doubt when poor Lyon was cut loose from the noose that he had breathed his last. Barlinnie executions were horrific and repellent occasions but they were carried out in workmanlike fashion. The condemned man fell through a trap door into a room below which was conveniently near the mortuary. He then dangled long enough to make sure death had occurred. According to one *Herald* report, hanging has not always been such an efficient method of killing. For a while it was the practice to let relatives of the victim try to revive the still-warm corpse. If they succeeded the criminal was allowed to go home. Argyll prison records show that one Archie McPhun, hanged in Inveraray jail, was being rowed across Loch Fyne by his relatives when he stirred and resumed life. Even in the days of legal killing of criminals there was always a large percentage of the population against it. Long-time *Herald* columnist Jack McLean tells of the occasion when as an 11-year-old on holiday in England he asked his father, a stern Calvinist, 'Is this the day they hang Manuel?' McLean Senior made what the columnist called an uncharacteristic reply: 'It was a terrible thing which this poor man did, son. But God have mercy on him: we are doing worse.'

The death penalty has always had sinister trappings: the black cap worn by the judge; the grim notices pinned on jail gates; and the flying of a black flag at the prison on the day of death. The authorities ended the practice of the black flag when executions were moved to Barlinnie, and the death of John Lyon was marked only by a typewritten notice pinned on the prison gate at 8.15 a.m. reading: 'We the undersigned hereby declare that sentence of death was this day executed on John Lyon, in the prison of Barlinnie, in our presence.' The document was signed by two magistrates, Bailie James Duff and Bailie James Fraser; Robert Richmond, deputy town clerk; J P Mayo, the Governor; Dr Scott, the medical officer; and the chaplain, the Rev John Campbell. The *Herald* that day said the police had held up about 70 people who had come to view the statement posted 100 yards from the gate. After the main party had left the prison the spectators were allowed to approach the gates. The hanged man's younger brother and others of his relatives were among those who read the notice. Later Mr Mayo gave evidence at an inquiry before Sheriff Macdiarmid that the sentence was carried out at two minutes past eight on 8 February and the body buried within the prison precinct. Bailie Duff gave evidence that he had asked the prisoner if he was John Lyon and if he had anything to say. Lyon merely gave his name.

A mere two months later the Hanging Shed was back in action. This time it was Patrick Carraher's turn to walk the final eight steps across the landing to the gallows. Carraher seemed a man destined for the rope. He was convicted of stabbing John Gordon of Aitken Street, Glasgow, in the neck. His appeal against the death sentence failed, as did a petition to save his life – perhaps not so surprising considering that he had already been before the High Court twice on charges of murder. On the first occasion he was convicted of culpable homicide and jailed for three years, and he was subsequently jailed for three years for using a lethal weapon in an assault. So much for the reforming effect of prison.

Today Glasgow still has the type of hard man who glories in his own reputation, the sort of man who enjoys the sense of fear his presence brings to any gathering. It's nothing new. The year 1950 saw the hanging of Paul Christopher Harris in a celebrated case. Paul was said to enjoy a reputation as the fighting man of the district. His story had been largely forgotten for more than 40 years until the *Herald*'s revelation that the Hanging Shed was to be removed because of prison modernisation. Paul Harris' daughter Mary McCallum wanted to find out where her father's body lay. Research by the *Herald* indicated that the bodies of ten men who died on the Barlinnie gallows were buried side by side, wrapped in rough hessian, along the outside of D Hall. Sometime in the 1960s after capital punishment was removed from the statute books the plaques bearing the names of the dead had been removed. As part of the capital punishment ritual the victims of the gallows were denied civilised burial. Their bodies were covered in quicklime and buried in unconsecrated ground. All the evidence points to Harris lying with others including Lyon and Carraher and Peter Manuel, whose tale is told elsewhere in this book.

The story of Harris and his brother Claude says much about the Glasgow slums of the '40s and '50s. The brothers had been convicted of acting in concert to kill Martin Dunleavy of Neptune Street. Both had records. And both were sentenced to hang. But Paul confessed to the crime, a somewhat dodgy confession that was criticised by a Scottish Home Department official as 'couched in sanctimonious platitudes not to be expected of a man of Harris' type'.

Dodgy or not, it was enough to help the Scottish Secretary postpone Claude's execution for several days while Paul's eve-of-execution statements were considered. This resulted in a reprieve. Prison records of the time show that both the brothers had behaved with some dignity in the final days and even appeared to have won some sympathy from the prison staff. Paul played the hard man right to the end, jokingly reminding his brothers who visited him in the death cell to 'be smiling at 8 o'clock'. Sadly he went to the gallows with his arms pinioned by officers who were strangers rather than the men who had sat through the deathwatch with him. The view that the brothers had not acted in concert had been upheld despite Dunleavy's deathbed assertion that more than one man had been involved. It was a tawdry end to a tenement fight in the worst of Glasgow slums. Only later did Mary McCallum learn of her father's fate. But when she did – as a youngster of 12 or 13 – it was a revelation that blighted the rest of her life. Perhaps finding her father's unmarked grave finally brought her some peace.

Young John Lyon, the first to die on the Barlinnie gallows, was only 21 when he paid for his crime. But the last person to hang in Barlinnie was even younger – 19-year-old Tony Miller, labelled by the Press of the day as 'The Boy Killer'. Miller had been convicted on 16 November 1960 of the capital murder of John Cremin, a middle-aged homosexual, in the Queen's Park recreation ground on the southside of the city. Miller and an accomplice had been charged with the murder of Cremin, who had been hit on the head with a piece of wood and robbed of his watch, bank book, knife and £67. The area of the attack was a known haunt of homosexuals and Cremin had been an easy victim for two fit young men. Both pleaded not guilty but the accomplice claimed that Miller had struck the fatal blow.

Miller's lawyer Len Murray set up an appeal against the sentence of death. In a book published in 1995, Mr Murray recalled that one of the grounds for appeal was that the judge, Lord Wheatley, had failed to offer the jury the option of culpable homicide – an option which did not carry the death penalty. But the court of appeal refused to act and set the execution for just three days before Christmas. At this time there was growing revulsion in the country over the death penalty and a petition organised by Miller's family collected no fewer than 30,000 signatures. This was sent to the Scottish Secretary John S Maclay, and the reply came on December 19. With regret, Mr Maclay was unable to find sufficient grounds to justify him advising Her Majesty to interfere with the due course of the law. Hour after hour of sitting at petition tables in the city centre seeking the help of thousands of Christmas shoppers were to no avail. Back in the Bar-L the teenager was resigned to his fate. His mother visited him every afternoon but he refused to talk about the crime. 'It's too late now,' he said. And so the last person to hang in Barlinnie went to his death.

3

GODFATHERS AND
GOD FATHERS

Back in June 1999 a 71-year-old man hobbled from Glasgow Sheriff Court virtually unnoticed after admitting possessing cannabis worth £15. Walter Norville had heard the Crown accept his plea of not guilty to being concerned in the supply of amphetamine. Mr Norville's defence lawyer told the court that the elderly man 'was acutely embarrassed about being connected with drugs'. The accused was said to be very anti-drugs and to be helping on a voluntary basis with a drug rehabilitation programme in the city. The lawyer said that Norville had once made 'banner headlines' but now lived a quiet life and had become a great-grandfather. He suffered a lot of pain from arthritis and was on medication and found that cannabis was a great pain-reliever.

In keeping with his new-found status of quiet man, Walter Norville left court accompanied by friends and refusing to comment. But it was all rather different back in the '70s when Norville dominated the Glasgow headlines in spectacular fashion under his original name of Walter Norval. Then, the man – who many say was Glasgow's first godfather of crime – was jailed for 14 years for armed robberies on a hospital payroll and a bank. These raids resulted in 13 men appearing in four separate trials, with six being acquitted and seven – including Norval, who emerged as the Mister Big of the operation – getting a total of 74 years in jail. Norval's had been a dramatic trial with armed police inside and outside the High Court. The four judges were given armed guards, such was the high profile of the case involving the Glasgow underworld. It was a real old-style Glasgow gangster occasion, with an overnight petrol-bombing at the North Court before the trial even began. Norval's daughter was cleared of the bombing and of intimidating witnesses, but her husband was jailed for five years.

Armed policemen, the possibility of witnesses intimidated and court-room tales of armed violence concocted an evil mixture. Of drugs and drug-dealing there was no mention. But that would change under the gangland rule of the men who followed Norval as Glasgow godfathers: men as violent and as dangerous as any in the criminal history of the city, but who grew fat on the vast profits to be made out of controlling the distribution of drugs and spreading the misery of addiction and death.

Arthur Thompson's bulky frame was familiar to anyone who spent much time socialising in Glasgow in the 1980s. At fund-raising dinners he was a figure of menace, despite his uniform of smart business suit, collar and tie, and expansive smile. He wore his fearsome reputation with the honour of a Corleone who had suddenly found himself in the cold rain-swept Far West of Europe. The smart dress-code went with his image of himself as a businessman. Until his death, ironically of natural causes in the spring of 1993 at the age of 62, he denied that he was Glasgow's Godfather. He consistently said that he was just a businessman and on his death his lawyer, the legendary defender Joe Beltrami, said they had had an 'excellent business relationship' for more than 30 years. And when the alleged criminal overlord sued a Sunday newspaper that had linked him with crime in Glasgow, and won a substantial out-of-court settlement, he gave half the sum to the Cash for Kids appeal run by Radio Clyde. This action, said Joe Beltrami, summed up his client.

However, few businessmen had his string of convictions for extortion, robbery, housebreaking and reset. Or indeed links with

London gangsters like the Krays and Mad Frankie Fraser. Even fewer had a son like Arthur Jnr who was jailed for 11 years for trying to control the Glasgow drug scene. Young Arthur died a violent death in August 1991 when he was shot and killed outside his home while on leave from Noranside Prison. The bullet-riddled bodies of two underworld figures – Bobby Glover and Joe 'Bananas' Hanlon – were found in a car on the morning of young Thompson's funeral. Both were alleged to be associates of Paul Ferris, a man who features later in this book. But it was Thompson Snr who was arguably the most prominent figure in the Scottish underworld since the Second World War. Despite the fact that he had not faced a jury in the 30 years before his death, and only served brief jail sentences, there is no doubt that he headed up a criminal clan involved in protection rackets and latterly drugs.

In death, both the Thompsons had the trappings of the Mafia – funeral motorcades with lashings of flowers and neatly dressed men waiting on the streets to pay their final respects. One measure of Thompson's place in the Glasgow underworld was the rash of stories that emerged immediately after his death. These speculated on violent feuds between warring parties wanting to take control of the crime scene. One senior police officer said: 'There could be bloody warfare. There's an empire loaded with dough to be fought over, and there are a lot of hard neds desperate to get their hands on it. We expect things to be quiet for a spell while plans are formalised and made ready to be put into action. Then all hell could be let loose. We will be watching closely.' Events proved such speculation to be something of an underestimate!

A heart attack had killed Arthur, a 'businessman' who had survived three murder attempts. His luxury home, something of a fortress, in Provanmill Road near the notorious housing estate of Blackhill, was a major East End landmark. Few had not heard of the Ponderosa and the thousands of pounds spent on it in dubious taste, and many feared its flamboyant inhabitants. After his death his wife stood on the doorstep of this fortress, tear-stained with cigarette in hand. Too upset to speak, she was turning away callers from the door. Mrs Rita Thompson was no stranger to death and violence. More than a year earlier young Arthur had died in a blaze of gunfire. And her own mother had died in the first attempt to kill Arthur Snr in 1966 when a bomb blew their car apart. But the Godfather seemed destined to die in his bed – 20 years later in another attempt on his life he was shot in a city bar. He went to hospital for treatment but refused to co-operate with the police – another nod of the head in the direction of the Mafia and the memorable story of the Chicago gangster arriving at a hospital bleeding to death from bullet wounds and asking the cops: 'Who's been shot?'

Another attempt on Thompson's life came in 1990 when he was pinned against a fence by a car, breaking a leg. The police were not officially informed of this little incident, but it was further strong evidence that he had many enemies – something he liked to deny, telling one reporter: 'I have more friends than Hitler had an army.' By a strange coincidence a heart attack also claimed the life of one of his most notable associates, John 'Blind Jonah' McKenzie, though in this case drug abuse was suspected. McKenzie was a Glasgow thug who had the dubious distinction of being accused of a gangland murder while being blind in both eyes. He was jailed in 1985 for five years after being caught in the East End with a massive consignment of heroin. 'Blind Jonah' had lost the sight of one eye as a young man, and he lost the second when he was allegedly stabbed in the face by the aforementioned Joe "Bananas" Hanlon, a gangland rival. But the death of Arthur Thompson Snr was not the end of the story of his clan and their involvement in crime. The future was to bring further evidence of their sinister control of crime in Glasgow, though it was a control bitterly contested by a new breed of criminal, more sophisticated but no less evil.

One of the joys of *The Herald* archive is its comprehensiveness. A browse around the vile deeds of various Thompsons also brings you the uplifting stories of Godfathers of a different kind.

Bill Christman was on the face of it an unlikely candidate to become a Barlinnie legend. From Joplin, Missouri, his first job was selling rhythm-and-blues records to fans of that particular genre of music. But he was not destined to spend his life behind the counter of a music store. A summer break in West Virginia 'where poverty was so dreadful it turned my values upside-down' was followed by a slow recovery from a bout of pneumonia which provided some real thinking time. The decision was taken to study for the ministry; a friend mentioned Edinburgh and the idea of studying far from home was appealing. If he studied in Scotland and decided to pack it in after a while it would create no big ripples back in the States. But he stayed the course and found himself a minister in Niddrie, one of the capital's most depressed areas. Four years later he went back across the Atlantic on a prestigious scholarship to Harvard. But a call from Scotland changed his life again. The invitation was to minister in Easterhouse – an area with its own problems of crime and poverty, but with a strong mix of decent folk doing their best for their families in difficult conditions.

Bill Christman decided to accept the challenge. All that was missing was the airfare, but his fellow students had a whip-round to solve that problem. 'Maybe they wanted to get rid of me,' he joked. His seven years in Easterhouse coincided with a period when the area's gangs were getting maximum publicity in the local Press. Nonetheless he got on fine, perhaps helped by his accent that was by now 'half American hill-billy and half Easterhouse', and at one stage he was running five football teams for young gang-members and potential members. This attempt to show that there was more to life than violence and aggression was on the whole pretty successful and Bill was able to tell an interviewer that 'only one boy in any of these teams ever got into more trouble'.

The next stop in a fascinating career was Lansdowne Church in the West End of the city, which, unlike Easterhouse, is an area where the grim shadow of Barlinnie isn't a dominating feature. According to Bill, the challenge here was 'trying to build multi-faith bridges with a community of many religions and with the support of the congregation. I learned how difficult it was to build these bridges when at that time, people had not yet come together as a community.' After the West End of Glasgow came five years as minister of a new congregation of St Columba's in Ayr, created by the merging of three churches – a situation that brought its own problems. His time in Ayr ended when he heard about the new post as full-time prison chaplain. He applied and won the appointment. 'At each post along the way I learned something that matters,' says this man of God.

So an American-born minister became the Church of Scotland's first full-time prison chaplain. Whether visiting the Bar-L or any one of Scotland's prisons, Bill had a golden rule for his new role. 'Regardless of what the crime involved is, I don't want to know the details of why any man or woman was sent to prison before I meet them. I am human like anyone else, and I could be prejudiced – and that is something I must try hard to avoid.' Bill, who acquired the nickname 'The Godfather' in Easterhouse, saw his role as supporter of the long-established part-time chaplains. Much of the work involved him visiting relatives on the outside when a prisoner has worries. Letters from a loved one can stop coming, leaving the prisoner in the dark about what is happening to the important people in his life. Sorting out such matters is all in a day's work for a man who liked to mix and talk in the streets with late-night people. Bill so often got to the scene of the trouble that one chief constable gave him a card to carry, explaining to policemen on the beat exactly who he was! Handy when he ran a soup kitchen in George Square.

Along with his Roman Catholic colleagues, Bill and the other chaplains had to work within the rules and regulations of the prison service but preserve a total confidentiality. One interviewer told him that some prisoners see the chaplain as a soft mark, asking, 'Are you one?' The answer was devastatingly honest. 'Maybe sometimes, but so often there can be a hidden reason why a prisoner really seeks your help and you've got to find what might be there.'

A Godfather of yet another kind was Bill McGibbon who graduated from gangland to the God squad. Bill served a stretch in the Bar-L for attempted murder, but as he lay in his cell he had a dream – a dream that one day when he was a free man he would return to spread the word of God among the inmates. It was a dream he turned into reality, and in 1993 he told his story of going back into prison to tell the hard cases that 'Jesus loves them even if their mothers don't.' Bill was a founding member of the Scottish Offenders project, a group that bought a flat in Glasgow's southside to help rehabilitate ex-prisoners, especially lifers. Bill grew up in Bridgeton in the East End, a favourite playground for the razor gangs. Although he had day jobs in the meat market and work in a shipyard by night, he ran with the infamous Baltic Fleet and the Brigton Derry. 'Your razor went everywhere with you,' he was quoted as saying. His conversion started with Bible classes in Barlinnie. The conversion of others who had gone down the wrong track followed.

There is a modicum of humour to be found in the *Herald's* tales of prison-life down the years, a classic example coming from a recent Diary entry on Father Jim Lawlor – one of the Catholic chaplaincy team at Barlinnie. Father Lawlor was visiting a youngster recently admitted. The new boy was not too happy about this visit from a Catholic priest, but in an effort to put him at his ease Jim asked his age. 'I'll be 17 in two weeks,' was the answer. 'Oh,' said the priest, 'that means we are both Capricorns.' 'Not me, mate,' said the new inmate – 'I'm a Protestant.'

One of the great Barlinnie characters was Father Willy Slavin, who pops up in the files in all sorts of roles from long-distance cyclist to co-ordinator of the Scottish Drugs Forum, as well as spending ten years as the prison's Catholic chaplain. Few knew more about prison and drugs than Father Slavin and he accused the courts of filling prisons with addicts. His belief was that drug-users needed help, not to be banged-up in prison. In his view, in the early '90s no significant resources were being put into tackling drug addiction by the Scottish Prison Service, a view not shared, of course, by the Scottish Office.

Father Slavin underlined his beliefs when around the same time the *Herald* ran a fantasy spending-spree series exploring what wealth meant to different people. The outspoken priest was concerned that no premises were then available when addicts needed them – at 2 a.m. 'I would buy a city-centre block and provide a centre which is open when everything else closes down at 5 p.m. You could maybe call it a nine-to-five centre. It would give access to all the mainstream services with doctors, nurses, social workers, maybe a dentist on call as well as the police and a cafe. It would be providing statutory services but on flexi-time. Normally these services start at 9 a.m. when many people who wander the city-centre at night are trying to put their heads down.

'The police tell us there are a whole lot of people walking about the city at 3 a.m. Many don't know where they are going and, now that the licensing hours have been extended, there is a lot of alcohol swilling around at that time. We know that there are kids who will not go to casualty although they have bullet wounds.

'The homeless scene in Glasgow is getting noisier. The Talbot Centre and the Allan Centre can only mop up a certain number. It might be possible to have places where people can sleep through the night because police stations are now being used for that. Drug-workers and homeless workers say they need a city-centre crisis centre, but I feel that it would be twice as valuable if it operated at night.'

One man's dream and a picture of the desperation on the streets around ten years ago. All the more poignant today, when at the beginning of the new millennium the evil trade in drugs can raise enough anger to bring thousands of protesters on to the streets and the papers rant against teenage beggars who proliferate on the city pavements.

4

THE HOOFER, THE PETERMAN
AND A SCRIBBLER

The Herald files feature many an unlikely juxtaposition of character and place, but none more striking than the story of 'Mr Moonlight'. One of Britain's top entertainers, Frankie Vaughan liked to dance on to a stage complete with straw boater and cane, make a few high-kicks and belt out a repertoire of songs that had his army of fans – mostly ladies of a certain age – almost swooning with delight. His polished stage persona was a million miles away from the deprivation and despair of Easterhouse in the '50s and '60s. In the days before the charts were dominated by boy bands and girl groups, and even groups manufactured on TV, Frankie had a series of hits – 'Green Door', 'Garden of Eden', 'Kisses are Sweeter than Wine' and 'Give me the Moonlight', – the last of which spawned his nickname and became his signature tune. He also starred with Marilyn Monroe in the film 'Let's Make Love' as well as becoming the first British singer to feature in Las Vegas, long before Tom Jones and Engelbert Humperdinck.

But Frankie never forgot his own early days in Liverpool, which were as alien to the glitter and glamour of Vegas as life in Easterhouse. He was born Frank Abelson in his Russian grandmother's house. She still retained a heavy accent and liked to call the young Frank, her first grandson, 'my number vorn' – the origin of his stage name. Frankie is said to have topped the bill at every major British theatre at one time or another, and work often brought him to Glasgow where he learned of a particularly bad outbreak of young-gang violence in Easterhouse. The dapper theatrical decided to try to do something to help. In 1968 he managed to persuade many of the hard men of Easterhouse – then the biggest housing estate in Europe – to lay down their arms and stop the gang battles. Along with others he set up the Easterhouse Project, designed to keep youngsters off the streets, and staged a week-long show at the old Alhambra Theatre to raise funds for a youth club in the deprived area. It was a spectacular and unlikely intervention in the Glasgow war against crime. But it worked.

Thirty-two years later, in January 2000, official documents were released giving Frankie credit for helping to curb the violence in the then notorious estate. Papers that were part of a study undertaken by Glasgow University's School of Social Studies into gang activity in the city showed that when Mr Moonlight intervened, crime dropped dramatically. The papers had been kept from the public under a 30-year rule. But there it was in black and white: the story of the success of the Easterhouse Project in figures gathered by researchers from police records of assaults and robberies in the Northern Division – a marked dip after the singer became involved.

Sadly, this official accolade emerged after Frankie's death in September 1999 following heart surgery. In his later years the entertainer had considerable health problems, even being forced to quit a London West End hit because of them. The acknowledgement of his success was important, for down the years he had been the victim of carping criticism from some business leaders who believed that his high-profile intervention into the local community's affairs had helped to perpetuate an image of the scheme as a place no entrepreneur would choose to start a business. An odd viewpoint. Should good people just have stood aside and let the gangs tear lumps out of each other for eternity? At least Frankie mucked in and took considerable personal risk in stopping violent, bloody battles.

A more human assessment came on his death from Easterhouse councillor Jim Coleman, who told *The Herald*: 'Frankie Vaughan will always be fondly remembered by the people of Easterhouse. The Easterhouse Project is still doing good work and will serve as a tribute to his memory. Frankie got a tremendous reception from local people last year [1998] when he was a guest at the opening of the extension to the Easterhouse shopping centre. He gave the people a rendition of "Give me the Moonlight" and they all joined in.' And Easterhouse was no one-off effort for the singer: Frankie Vaughan had long campaigned for young people's charities – famously assigning record royalties to the National Association of Boys' Clubs. He regarded his fundraising work for children as 'an investment in the future'. His death brought warm tributes from showbusiness. He was a staunch supporter of the Variety Club and its Chief Barker Pip Burley said of him and his fund-raising: 'He was a showbiz legend, very generous and a wonderful supporter of the club who was always there when we needed him.' Fellow entertainer Des O'Connor summed him up fondly: 'Onstage he was dynamic. Offstage he was a gentleman and a friend, always ready to help anyone.' Sentiments that play well in Easterhouse.

But a lone effort, however worthy, was never going to solve the problems of a scheme like Easterhouse. The Rev Ron Ferguson, now at St Magnus Cathedral, Orkney, and a popular *Herald* columnist, was a minister in Easterhouse in the '80s when many of the old problems had emerged. In an interview he made the pertinent point that the economic and political problems that blighted such areas had never been tackled. 'Schemes like Easterhouse, Castlemilk and Drumchapel were like Soweto. They were places where people at the bottom of the pile were put. They were convenient and people were very happy to have others corralled there. The key thing, it always seemed to me, was to have jobs that would give people some dignity and worth. But there was no real investment. The New Towns got more resources and they were much more glamorous and exciting. 'There was also a sense in which schemes like Easterhouse were easy vote-fodder. The Labour party in the west of Scotland sometimes had a born-to-rule mentality – in the same way the Tory party in the south of England had – and any challenges to that authority were not welcomed.' A neat summing-up of a problem beyond the help of one person. But Frankie Vaughan did something. And some of what he wanted to happen, happened.

Another character and Glasgow legend, but of a very different kind, was Johnny Ramensky. Johnny was a habitual lawbreaker who in a career as a 'peterman' – a burglar skilled in safebreaking (and no-one was more skilled in this area than Johnny) – managed to get himself sentenced to more than 50 years in jail. Despite this, Ramensky became a figure held in some affection by those of his fellow citizens who hadn't had a safe blown by this king of the petermen. Some of this was because of his personality. He was nicknamed 'Gentle Johnny' by newspapers and police because he seldom if ever resisted arrest and once the cuffs were on he was quick to talk about his crimes. He was in fact often a victim of his own success. He was so skilled that every time he pulled a job the detectives were quick to recognise the sophistication of the safebreaking. Only one man could have done it. Suspicion fell on Johnny and mostly he was the guilty man.

In his various jail terms Johnny Ramensky had quite an effect on the prison service. Scottish Office files opened to the public in 1994 revealed that his efforts to escape from jail back in the 1930s had resulted in him being slapped in iron shackles to prevent other attempts at freedom. When the Secretary of State heard that 'Gentle Johnny' had been shackled he ordered a review of the prison service, and the barbaric practice of using leg-irons as a restraint was abolished.

Ramensky's concern not to cause unnecessary bother was demonstrated in 1938 when he was held in prison for a safe job. He wrote to the governor that he was 'anxious that care should be taken' in handling the smaller of two safes he had robbed. He didn't want anyone injured by the gelignite left behind. He was also held in affection by the public for his war service. In time of conflict, a man who didn't need a key to get into safes holding the enemy's secrets was valuable. Johnny was parachuted behind enemy lines to work for the secret service. In this he was a great success, but sadly after the Second World War the old habits returned and he again found himself behind bars. Strangely, his skills in wartime were acknowledged but in peace time there was more reluctance to use him in the fight against crime. The record released in 1994 showed that a bid by an Edinburgh professor of forensics to have his safebreaking skills recorded for posterity on film was turned down by the Lord Advocate.

Almost inevitably, 'Gentle Johnny' died while serving a sentence. He was 67 and in Perth prison after being found hiding on a roof in Ayr with intent to steal. Taken ill, he was transferred to hospital and died. The sadness in the life of this remarkable man, whose bravery served his country well in wartime, was that when peace arrived he couldn't settle down to a life on the right side of the law.

As demonstrated by the Frankie Vaughan story, told earlier in this chapter, Glasgow's great and good have a habit of shooting the messenger when some ugly facet of life in the city makes news. How's this for telling it like it is: 'It is a novel of tremendous power, a horrible story that holds one enchained in a shocked fascination from the moment of the drunken father's awakening in the first chapter to the razor-king's death at the iron-shod boots of his supplanters in the last. . . . The author is . . . unfalteringly realistic.' This comment came from the then *Glasgow Herald's* reviewer's verdict on Alexander McArthur and H Kingsley Long's novel *No Mean City*. Realistic or not, the city fathers were horrified and took the view that such a book only perpetuated the city's image of an evil wasteland haunted by gangs of razor-slashers. The book was banned from the city libraries on its publication in

1935. And the same controversy was running in the 1990s when there was a suggestion that McArthur should be belatedly honoured for his novel. Labour group leader Pat Lally, who grew up in the Gorbals, called it 'a distorted work of fiction'.

The fact is that *No Mean City* became a huge bestseller and continued in print for more than 50 years. But all that was little consolation to McArthur. One rumour had it that he committed suicide by jumping in the Clyde, allegedly full of remorse for the effect that his epic had had on the city. The truth is rather different. In September 1947 a couple of beat coppers came across the soaking wet body of a man near Rutherglen Bridge. To begin with they thought that he had clambered out of the Clyde, but when taken to the Royal Infirmary he died as a result of poisoning – he had swallowed a bottle of disinfectant. He had vomited all over himself, and was wringing wet – possibly the source of the drowning rumour – and was identified from a ration book. In his pocket was the sum of one shilling and three pence in cash – about six pence today.

This was the shabby end of the man behind *No Mean City*. McArthur was born in the Gorbals in 1901 and for many years lived in Waddell Street with his mother and brother. A baker by trade, he became unemployed and tried his hand at writing. Using slum life as a basis for fiction, he sent a couple of novels to London publishers Longmans. Neither was deemed worth publishing, but the subject-matter appealed to the publishers' readers and they commissioned the journalist H Kingsley Long to ghost-write a novel with McArthur – with the professional getting 75 per cent of the royalties and the ex-baker a mere 25 per cent.

The Herald was not alone in acclaiming the book as a powerful, realistic view of hard life in Rutherglen Road, Thistle Street, Hospital Street, Crown Street – where the central character razor-king Johnny Stark lived – and McArthur's own Waddell Street. It was an immediate success, despite the antagonism of the city fathers who seemed blind to the realities of life in the slums. The

Herald files show that down the years, a favourite ploy of feature-writers was to return to the Gorbals battlefields and speak to the people who lived the experience – the people who shared the pride and poverty of tenement life, the people who feared the gangs and the razor-slashers, the people who watched the battles on Glasgow Green. And, unsurprisingly, the general verdict of the eyewitnesses of the time is that McArthur got it right. His story of life on the south bank of the Clyde in the 1920s may not have been accurate in every last detail, but it came close enough to the truth to make it a valid piece of social history that can't be ignored.

But it seems that McArthur made little real money from his epic and his career as a writer foundered. Most of his contemporaries seem to think that, despite having an ear for Glasgow dialect, he was simply a bad writer. Indeed, despite sending reams of unsolicited material to all the Glasgow news-papers, little was published. He laboured on four novels, two plays and 20 short stories after the success of *No Mean City*, but the files suggest that only one short story was published – though a novel which was ghost-written appeared after his death.

Round the corner, mere yards from where the fictional Johnny Stark swaggered with his fearsome razor, there is now one of the most acclaimed theatres in Europe – the Citizens'. Nightly in winter the douce folk of the West End on the north side of the river, and residents of nearby schemes alike, turn out to watch innovative world-class performances, sipping chilled wine in the intervals. Is it too much to think that the labours of an out-of-work baker all these years ago helped to expose the horrors of poverty and low life in stinking slums, and contributed to the turn-around that now sees the Gorbals in renaissance, an area of desirable housing and pleasant living? The city fathers of the 1930s and some of a more modern hue think so, but they are wrong.

5

THE BRIGTON BILLY BOYS
AND STREET-FIGHTING GIRLS

You tend to hear a lot about good fellas with hearts of gold in the chronicles of gangsterdom. The Mafia dons loved their mothers and showed respect for the family as well as the Family. The Krays, at the end of their careers, were presented by some sections of the media as some kind of London East End Robin Hoods in fedoras and two-piece suits. Similar hogwash is often spouted about the Glasgow gangs of the 1920s and '30s – they only fought among themselves and the general public had little to fear from them. Angry men with hatchets, razors, bicycle chains and broken bottles were always dangerous. And the living relatives of shopkeepers terrorised into providing financial support for such as the Billy Boys and Norman Conks will confirm that the totally innocent were at risk from the pitched battles of the gangs.

The names of the gangs are intriguing. The Billy Boys has an obvious link with King Billy and Orangism. The source of the name of their main rivals, the Norman Conks, has often caused speculation in the columns of *The Herald*: one theory has it that it simply came from the Norman Street area and the word 'conquerors'. Other infamous gangs included the South-Side Stickers, the Butney Boys (from Maryhill), and the Calton Entry.

You often hear stories of 'square goes', when a single villain slugged it out with a cop. It did happen and there was, in fact, a pre-war cop nicknamed PC Hitler who used his fists in fair fights to control the thugs on his patch. But this was exceptional. Generally the gangs used chains and cut-throat razors in their battles with their enemies, mostly for control of turf. Their exploits were often far from fair fights. King Billy Fullerton, leader of perhaps the most infamous of the gangs, the Bridgeton Billy Boys, was jailed for 12 months in 1931 for leading a group of around 40 people in an attack on five police constables. Long odds against the boys in blue.

The Billy Boys had been formed in 1924 after a football match between some Bridgeton boys and youngsters in a team called Kent Star, based in the Calton. It is ironic that to this day, despite valiant efforts from the clubs, football can still spark large-scale sectarian violence. Young Fullerton, later to be named King Billy for his control of the largest, most violent of the gangs, claimed that he had been attacked with a hammer after scoring the winning goal. Along with around 30 of his friends he created the Billy Boys in a bid for bloody revenge. The Billy Boys were active into the 1930s and at one time they are said to have had about 800 adherents. As chronicled elsewhere in this book, the vigorous activities of the police under the legendary Chief Constable Sir Percy Sillitoe eventually eradicated the worst excesses of the gangs. The Billy Boys were, of course, Orange sympathisers. Anyone who believes that Catholics living in their fiefdom were unaffected by the doings of this gang of thugs has a distorted view of reality – especially in the years when King Billy was the dominant figure in the East End.

In later years, with the gangs on the run, Fullerton showed another side of his colours by becoming a section 'captain' in Oswald Mosley's fascist movement, leading a battalion of 200 which was used to attack and disrupt the political left wing. He was also said to have been a paid police informer. Another measure of this street-fighting man's political leanings is that in the real battles of the Second World War, he was a conscientious objector. There is little in his story to mitigate a life of violence, but there is a curious footnote in the archives about an incident near the end of his life. The man who had led the anti-Catholic thugs of the Billy Boys with bloody ruthlessness carried the legendary boxer Peter Keenan across the turf of Celtic Park to celebrate a win in the ring. Indeed, Fullerton worked at the end of his life as a ring-whip for the boxer/promoter much loved in Glasgow and known usually and affectionately as PK. The name ring-whip harked back to the violence of bare-knuckle boxing. In the days before stadia and artificial boxing rings the fighters each had their own whips to control their supporters, though in time the term really only came to mean a sort of super-steward.

William Fullerton died in July 1962 aged 57. A crowd of around 1000 gathered outside a Bridgeton tenement to watch the funeral party set out. *The Herald* reported that 'at Bridgeton Cross, scene of many affrays between the Billy Boys and the rival Roman Catholic gang the Norman Conks, led by Bull Bowman, traffic was stopped as the funeral moved from Fullerton's home in Brook Street by way of Crownpoint Road to Riddrie cemetery. A strong force of police was present to control the crowds'. Old habits die hard, and though the Billy Boys had passed into history the procession was led from Brook Street to Fielden Street by a flute band. The violence that was so much a part of the Fullerton legacy lasted until the 1990s. King Billy's son, also named William, was found slumped over a car's steering wheel in James Street, Bridgeton in 1994 and died in the Royal Infirmary. He had been stabbed. Fullerton Jnr's own son, again called William, had been shot in the leg at close range in the Candleriggs 18 months earlier.

An intriguing picture of what it was like in the razor gangs was highlighted in an interview with Bill Gilvear, a gang member who was converted by a Tent Hall preacher called Seth Sykes. Bill had grown up in the Gallowgate in the direst of poverty, 'feet sticking out of our soles, not a ha'penny to rub together'. His father had been a convert of the Tabernacle Church in Maryhill but had died in an accident when Bill was only ten, and the family turned away from religion. But friends of his father kept working at Bill and indeed it was respect for his father's beliefs that finally lured him to the Tent Hall and that fateful meeting with Seth Sykes. Bill's conversion was the start of long years dedicated to Christianity. During the famous 1955 Billy Graham crusade in the city he worked every night as a counsellor. Graham and his adherents are credited with turning around the life of many a Glasgow hard man. Bill Gilvear, who had been a member of the 'Stick-it' gang at 14 and who remembers hiding up closes in the Gallowgate to dodge 'Holy Joes', had come a long way.

As a 14-year-old member of the Stick-it, he recollects the gang's *raison d'être* was to do its worst to their greatest rivals, the Santois. For many the Stick-it was a training ground for a stretch in the Bar-L – and for one member, a step on the road to the gallows. In 1991 Bill was described as a gentle figure with pebble glasses and wearing a sports jacket. He reached into the inside pocket of the jacket and told the interviewer: 'This is where you kept your bicycle chain hidden. You pulled it out and a member of a rival gang got it against his face. And you took a safety razor blade and split it in two and that gave you a long thin blade. You hid it in the edge of your cap and if someone said good evening to you, you could slit their throat from ear to ear. We were the terror of the eastside of Glasgow.' A disturbing portrait of a violent way of life told with sorrow by a man who had seen the light. Seth Sykes and the Tent Hall mission just off High Street – a massive engine of good for many years – had made an astonishing conversion. After he first accepted God into his life Bill had told fellow gang-members of his conversion. 'Ye stupid daft Holy Joe, you'll be back in a week.' Not so. Bill Gilvear went to Bible college, then spent years in Africa as a missionary and a lifetime wiping out his days in the Stick-it.

The Billy Boys may be the most infamous of the gangs, but they were only one of a massive total. It all seems to have started in the 1870s with the Penny Gang, said to have been given the name because they paid fines at a penny-a-week. One writer estimates that the city has had more than 600 gangs in the last 150 years, though that seems to be a measurement of the 'how long is a piece of string' school of mathematics. Many of the names of the older gangs have been passed from generation to generation. Bundy, Torran Toi, Drummy, Aggro and Skinheads were said to be still in use in the late 1990s, albeit as a loose definition of particular groups of thugs rather than highly organised gangs with a command structure.

Many of the gang names have curious derivation too. The Baltic Fleet, a Bridgeton gang that seems to have lasted in some form or other from the 1930s until the '90s, caused some discussion in the files in the late '80s. Any romantic notion that it commemorated some far-off sea battle was torpedoed. The reality is much more mundane – Baltic Street, the original home turf of the gang, got its name from the fact that the Baltic Jute Company of Dundee opened a factory there. Apparently it was opened with quite a flourish but failed and had to close down because of poor business. The gang seemed to last longer: it was mentioned in court in a stabbing case in 1997. That the gangs were still a serious problem in some areas was evidenced by the fact that Edgar Prais, QC, speaking for the defence in this case, said that in Easterhouse gang fights were staged 'like Saturday fixtures'.

In Easterhouse in 1996 the police ran a fierce campaign to clamp down on gang fights in the summer holidays. There were heavy 'disorder' patrols, involving marked and unmarked cars and 20 officers and mounted police. The Glaswegian talent for humour in the blackest of situations emerged when one teenager was asked if mounted policing was effective. He replied: 'Well, my mate's begonias are coming along well – his da's been using horse crap in the garden.' At least this is some measure of progress – it is difficult to imagine the Billy Boys or Norman Conks taking much of an interest in free fertiliser for their garden flowers.

In fact, this particular police exercise, christened 'Lone Ranger' by the gangs, was indeed effective. To begin with an average of 12 youths were arrested each night for disturbances, but that quickly fell to one or two. The weapons confiscated as a result of increased stop-and-search were disturbing – meat cleavers, machetes, butcher's knives and daggers among them. *The Herald* interviewed a tiny thug called Malcolm at this time, and his comments were revealing. Aged 15, he said he ran with the Drummy gang and had been in 'a few fights' using his fists and feet, maybe a bottle or his belt. He found himself arrested for beating up, along with his mate, a member of the Aggro gang. Unconcerned, he was rescued from the cells a few hours later by his mother, who merely remarked: 'You again, you bastard'. He was back on the streets a few hours later. One of his pals explained how fights begin. 'The Aggro give us grief. They just act wide-o, sing their gang names, so we attack.' Both these 15-year-olds told the reporter that they would have no hesitation in attacking a youngster from another scheme.

Back in the East End there were reports of pitched battles between the Shamrock from Royston and the Monks from Dennistoun. The areas on either side of the M8 seemed to spark many a fight, one report talking about a war-zone stretching from Sighthill and Roystonhill through Blackhill to Easterhouse, all on the north side, and from Riddrie through Cranhill to Barlanark on the south. In one incident the police helicopter was brought in to break up fighting between more than 40 youths in Balornock. There were even reports of thugs as young as eight being caught with axes. And across the river in Castlemilk a reporter found evidence of changes in the gang culture since the days of the Gorbals feuds. A member of the Machrie Fleeto said: 'We've no leader, its just all mates, nae colours either, it's no America.' It was claimed that these modern gangs didn't split on religious grounds and fights were claimed to take place without blades: 'hands and feet will dae us. Or maybe a cosh or baseball bat.' Changed days? But a youngster in the wrong place could still get hurt.

The contrast between the gangs of the 1930s and their successors is striking. Files recording the territorial battles of such as the Billy Boys and the Norman Conks make barely a mention of women: wives and sweethearts seemed there only to bind up the bloody wounds and weep in court or at the graveside. But 70 years later, violence is no longer the sole province of the young Glasgow male. As the 20th century ran out, the archive picked up more and more stories of female violence.

In the 1940s it was said that there were girl gangs such as the She Tongs, Young She Cumbies and Young She Tongs. But in the '90s Strathclyde Police were claiming that female gang membership only extended to a few hangers-on among the Queen Street Posse, a minor gang chiefly involved in shoplifting sprees. Nonetheless, Glasgow was not spared from the rise in female street crime seen throughout Britain. Reports testify to young women who would use a broken bottle or a lino knife on a man without a thought. Documentary film-maker Liz Ingram – who produced *Possil Girls – We Are Here* for Channel 4, a portrait of girls involved in shoplifting and group violence – said: 'What we found were rough girls who were quite happy to wade in. There exist girls who don't mind fighting and girls for whom fighting would be a most awful shock. Others can fight their friends and forget it. They can do it for a buzz'. Some sociologists believe that any rise in female crime is from a small base and much of it is drug-related and unreported. In reality the actual rise in female crime is hard to gauge from statistics that often don't differentiate between male and female. And while no-one could claim that the war against the gangs, male or female, has finally been won, the fact is that these days street violence is largely under control, despite sporadic outbreaks particularly in the schemes. Vigilance is still needed but the graph of gang warfare is going in the right direction.

It is interesting to note that when the late-night radio chat-show host Derek Jameson and his wife Ellen were given a programme based in Glasgow, as part of a BBC initiative to produce more national programmes from regional centres, he could say: 'We had our doubts. The image persists of Glasgow as a grim place of poverty and despair where gangs go around cutting each other up with razors.' This from a man who had edited Fleet Street newspapers! But after working in the city he was able to say: 'In the event we have never felt safer anywhere.' Rab C Nesbitt, that magnificent TV comic creation – Socrates in a string vest – says: 'Glasgow's a city that can be anything it chooses to be. I wish it would choose to be Monte Carlo.' The Jamesons could respond: 'Well, mate, we have news for you. We are just back from a holiday in Monte Carlo and, believe it or not, the city of culture is miles better.'

6

SO SPECIAL THEY
CLOSED IT DOWN

The Special Unit at Barlinnie – still talked about on the streets of Glasgow as the Nutcracker Suite or the Wendy House – helped swell the *Herald* archives from its opening in 1973 to its controversial closure in the mid-'90s. The achievements of this ground-breaking experiment in penal theory and the vehement antagonism of its critics – it was even said that a former Moderator of the Church of Scotland wanted it shut down – spawned thousands of words. Even to this day it stirs controversy. But there can be, to my mind at least, no doubt that its creation was visionary and that for a number of years it worked well. One of the brains behind the concept was a small, quiet Aberdonian called Ian Stephen. Now one of Scotland's leading forensic psychologists, he worked as a consultant on the hit TV series *Cracker* starring Robbie Coltrane. But he acknowledges the difference between TV crime and the reality: 'The *Cracker* character was really nothing like what real forensics is all about. You couldn't survive behaving in the extreme way he did – the police wouldn't use you.' That apart he observed that the series was an enormous success, attracting 14 million viewers, and that 'before *Cracker* the public hadn't heard of forensic psychology and the Press wasn't covering it. The drama brought it to the fore'.

No one knows more about the differences between TV crime and reality than Ian Stephen. He studied psychology at Aberdeen in the '60s but became disillusioned and took to teaching languages at a Borders school. That experience re-ignited his interest in psychology and he began working with young offenders in Glasgow. 'If you can work with these kids you can work with violent men,' he told one reporter. 'The kids are far worse.' The Barlinnie Special Unit helped to gain forensic psychology the respect of the authorities and Ian is proud of his work there. 'I was the only psychologist working in the Scottish prison system at the time. People were concerned because we didn't have the death penalty any more, and these men were going around stabbing and rioting and taking over jails . . . We said: "We don't know what we are going to do with them, let's try and set up this different unit and see where it goes". We were lucky having some strong men among the staff – and among the prisoners, people like Jimmy Boyle, who realised that this was their last chance. We used to have meetings that lasted for hours, which was about trying to resolve violence before it became physical. We didn't have cells, we didn't have punishment – instead we wanted to give the responsibility back to the prisoners. If you took it away they could blame the prison system for their violence.'

Ian Stephen had an ideal chance to compare textbook theories and the real criminal mind. And there were terrifying incidents. Convicted killer Larry Winters once threatened him when the two were alone in the Special Unit. The prisoner picked up a pair of scissors and said, 'Do you realise I could cut your throat? I have done this to better people than you. How do you feel?' The answer was 'scared' but Winters just laughed and threw the scissors down. Stephen's verdict on Winters was that he was a very violent man, very bright but with poor self-control. A dangerous mixture. Despite all his experience he finds that some cases are beyond understanding, and is on record as believing that child-killer Myra Hindley should never be released. 'Most murderers kill only once, but others do it for malicious intent, because of their own needs. You have got to be progressive when you can afford to be, but you can't afford to be stupid.' An observation that is particularly pertinent bearing in mind the eventual demise of the Unit. He went on to tell the reporter: 'You don't change people. What you do is to help them adapt, so that the things that were negative for them in the past can be channelled.'

From the start the Special Unit was a 'test bed'. A small group of long-term prisoners, generally serving 15 years or more, was held together in a secure area but with a much more relaxed regime than that faced by prisoners held in the normal cells. Prisoners wore their own clothes, had record-players and their own books. Freedom, responsibility and a degree of personal choice were all watchwords in an experiment that bucked the trend of normal prison hierarchy. Even mail was uncensored and the staff-to-prisoner ratio was high. The man considered by many to be the Unit's biggest success in reforming hard cases is Jimmy Boyle, once labelled by the Press as one of the most fearsome gangsters in Glasgow's history. He was found guilty of murder in 1967 and given life. He adapted to life behind bars with further violence against prison staff, and as a result endured long periods in solitary and spent time in the cells within cells, the infamous cages in Porterfield Prison, Inverness, a regime intended to break the spirit of the toughest. This brutal response to the problem of violent prisoners was temporarily abandoned in 1972, after one of the most violent disturbances in a Scottish prison in which five prison officers and four inmates, including Jimmy Boyle, were hurt. The cages reopened in 1978 before finally being dismantled in 1994.

In addition to Boyle, two other names tend to dominate the Special Unit story: Larry Winters and Hugh Collins. Winters and Boyle both sparked films, *Silent Scream* and *A Sense of Freedom*, which involved Glasgow actor David Hayman: he directed the Winters story and played Boyle in *A Sense of Freedom*. It is now largely forgotten, but the original concept of the film was the subject of great public criticism. Jeremy Isaacs, an independent producer in 1982, was commissioned to make the film. In a tribute to the late Bill Brown, the former Scottish Television chairman, Isaacs said: '*A Sense of Freedom* was a big film on a difficult subject, but Bill Brown bravely stood by me and the film-makers against a hostile press and public opinion.'

Winters was the Special Unit big name who never lived to see freedom. In 1997 he was found naked on a chamber pot dying of a drug overdose. A tragic end to the short life of a violent man who killed a barman for a fiver yet had an IQ of 160. Winters, like Boyle, was a troublesome prisoner. He attacked warders and got involved in rioting. He was moved from Peterhead to Barlinnie to join the experiment that was the Special Unit. Hayman's film of the Winters story, starring Edinburgh actor Iain Glen, won the Silver Bear award at the Berlin Festival and it was a source of anger for the director that not a penny for the venture came from Glasgow District or Strathclyde Regional Councils. The film had cost around £1 million to make and employed a high percentage of Scots. Three-quarters of the production cost had been spent in Glasgow. This lack of participation in a story highlighting crime once again brings into focus the almost traditional Glasgow city fathers' attitude of sticking their heads in the sand, even when the Special Unit could get worldwide publicity for an imaginative concept in penal reform. All the politicians could see was the portrayal of violence, not the treatment of it.

In Barlinnie, Winters met Bill Beech, a member of the so-called creative-artistic caucus who visited the Special Unit. As was intended to happen, the Unit gave Winters a sense of purpose and he began to write. Beech was quoted as saying: 'If Larry had lived, I think the writing would have flourished. That's the marvellous thing about the Unit. It was just a huge relief that he could actually sit down and write and relate to things. But the drugs he took masked all that. He was still in prison and facing the rest of his life there.'

The abuse of drugs is critical in the Special Unit story. In the case of Larry Winters it posed a lot of questions about the administering of tranquillisers in jail. The convicted killer had an extensive knowledge of drugs, and it is something of a mystery how a man who knew all about tolerance levels became so careless about his experiments with dosage that he killed himself. His death led to a public outcry about the role of drugs in the notoriously liberal regime in the Unit at that time. And there is no doubt that the use by inmates of drugs brought in from the outside had much to do with the eventual closure of the Unit. But before that happened, the Barlinnie project – and in particular the activities of the Unit's two most prominent members Jimmy Boyle and Hugh Collins – were to become the subject of detailed analysis in literally hundreds of news reports and features.

According to David Hayman, who so successfully played Boyle in *A Sense of Freedom*, he was 'a very different beast from Larry Winters. For one thing Jimmy was much more outgoing and socially oriented, as he has proved since his release, whereas Larry's journey was definitely inward.' Boyle, who went on to write *A Sense of Freedom* and *The Pain of Confinement* after his release, had spent 25 years in institutions until the Special Unit and his marriage to psychiatrist Sarah Trevelyan changed his life. The facts of his change in lifestyle are remarkable and an affront to some who hated the idea of an ex-con living in some style and luxury despite his reform to a legal and productive way of life. The memory of dirty protests in which walls were smeared with excrement was hard to forget.

Free, and an acclaimed sculptor, Jimmy Boyle made little attempt to placate his critics. He travelled the world for artistic commissions and drove around Edinburgh in a Rolls Royce said to have been given to him by a wealthy American in payment for a sculpture. In one interview he attacked head-on those who grudged him his material success: 'The only thing I can say about people like that is that they have allowed themselves to become prisoners of my past. I have moved on but they have allowed themselves to become stuck. My life has moved on beyond my wildest dreams. There is a thrawn jealous aspect to some people's attitude.' And there is more than the mere sybarite to the reformed Boyle, despite the love of fine wines and beautiful homes. Along with Sarah he got involved in working with young people, drawing on the Special Unit lessons about the therapeutic and empowering potential of art and working with former drug-users, the homeless and in HIV projects. And his new life was not without its own tragedy – his son James, from his first marriage, got involved in drugs and died in a stabbing. And in January 2001 he and Sarah confirmed that they had separated just a week before their 20th wedding anniversary, making the announcement in a statement from the Gateway Exchange Trust, a charity they run for problem youngsters in Edinburgh.

One of the biggest ironies in the Special Unit story is the conflict between Boyle and Hugh Collins, who also escaped into the art world after years of being caged. Collins, like Boyle, became a successful sculptor. In one interview he says: 'I was fortunate, I was no bad at it. When I had the idea to carve the statue of Christ I took it as a sign. This makes me sound like a maniac. It took me two years. But this is the bizarre thing; it was the best time of my life.' He said he saw the project as a 'punishment. A penance'. In addition to the sculptor's hammer and chisel, the word processor became an artistic weapon for him: his books *Autobiography of a Murderer* and *Walking Away* touch raw nerves.

Collins was jailed in 1975 for the gangland murder of a rival, Willie Mooney. And like Boyle's, his early years behind bars were troublesome – a dark mixture of stabbing warders, hunger-strikes, drug addiction and solitary confinement. He was exactly the sort of long-term prisoner the Special Unit was designed for and he was moved to Barlinnie. He is outspoken about his time there: 'The Special Unit saved me but it also tortured me. I was made into a pet lion for the social workers, psychologists and lawyers who came there. Some of it was disgusting. These people were like groupies. They patronised you, got a thrill from being near you.

Some of the women who visited the Unit would even sleep with you.' In *Walking Away* he controversially tries to explain his crimes. 'All violence is evil. Whether it is Myra Hindley killing children, me killing Willie Mooney, those kids killing Jamie Bulger, a British soldier shooting girl joy-riders in Ireland or the airforce bombing innocent Iraqis.'

Despite their animosity there is a striking similarity in the Boyle and Collins stories – at least until their past lives as prison tough-guys had receded. Boyle married a psychiatrist he met when inside; likewise Collins married artist Caroline McNairn after meeting her in jail. In some ways, though, Collins emerges as a more complex character. In one remarkable interview in the archives he discusses – in laceratingly honest fashion – his criminal days and what he has become. 'I was never a gangster,' he says, 'only a bampot.' And of his life of violence he says: 'The only person I can apologise to is dead. The only man who can forgive me is dead.' After stabbing Willie Mooney he spent 16 years in prison and in fear. 'I was afraid of death. I was afraid of rejection. I see now my violence was the product of fear.' This deep-thinking controversial man was, despite his cynicism, ideal fodder for the Special Unit. A talent for sculpture uncovered in the Bar-L changed his life, and in the Special Unit he also showed signs of the writing talent that he was to exploit so spectacularly and controversially on release. There is a strong feeling of self-loathing in his work. He aggressively denies accusations that his writing produces blood money. He says, 'I don't want to be a hero of the underworld. The books make me look horrible. I want to show how horrible violence is'.

These are the words of a Special Unit success, one of many criminals whose lives were turned around by this ground-breaking project. But as with any exercise in cutting new ground, the critics were vocal on the sidelines. In the case of the Special Unit, the outside opponents of the project were vociferous enough – though many of the critics were actually in the prison service itself. Back in 1994 Prisons Inspector Alan Bishop blasted the lifestyle in the Unit, then home to eight killers. He talked of prisoners being taken on shopping trips and visits to swimming pools. Cell security checks were said to be almost non-existent and it was claimed that visitors were not searched and stayed too long. It was also claimed that conditions were worse for the prison officers than the prisoners. Mr Bishop did not want the Unit closed but he wanted the system tightened up and returned to the original regime. At this time the Unit had been open for 21 years and there were constant allegations of inmates enjoying sex, booze and drugs while inside.

This particular report sparked a promise of a wide-ranging review from the then Tory Scots Secretary Ian Lang. Mr Bishop told a Press conference on his report that he had found no direct evidence of prisoners having sex with visitors or that drink or drugs were being taken during his inspection. But he could not rule out the possibility that these things were taking place. Mr Bishop wondered if 'liberalism had been taken too far. But for the lockable doors it would have been easy to forget this was a penal establishment.' Quite a big 'but', some might say. One of his main criticisms was that prisoners had come to believe that their stay in this unique part of the prison world was indefinite. He felt that this was very discouraging for other prisoners who might benefit from a spell in the Unit. For his part, Ian Lang said that the closure of the Unit was not desirable but he thought it appropriate to address its purpose and future. The writing was on the cell-block wall for all to read. And by the end of 1994 the project that had brought fame to the Scottish Prison Service was all but history.

The waves of criticism ended up swamping the once-celebrated experiment. But the prison service was facing the reality that the Unit had been blown off-course and that much of the criticism was valid. Edward Frizell, the service's chief executive, admitted at the time that there had been management failures and regular breaches of the trust that was a keystone of the experiment. However, the basic idea of small specialist units was to continue in acknowledgement of the Special Unit's long-term success in treating the most violent men in the prison community. A unit in Shotts was to continue as did the one in Perth, albeit with changes to the regime. The long-term plan was to eliminate the need for small units to handle difficult and disruptive prisoners, and an assessment centre at Shotts Prison was to play a major role. All this was wrapped up in a belated acceptance that the Special Unit had lost its way. The official view was that although the original purpose had been fulfilled, the service had taken its eye off the ball. Apart from all the introspective analysis by proponents and critics alike, the Barlinnie operation failed physical tests laid down by the working group who looked at the future of such units. It was claimed that the building was simply inadequate in some areas. The news of its demise attracted comment from every quarter. Ken Murray, a prison officer at the Unit during its first six controversial years, said he had read the closure report with a mixture of anger and sadness.

A couple of years after the closure *The Herald* ran a feature with the heading 'Hope amid all the Hatred' which said much about the Special Unit. Written by the Rev Ron Ferguson, a former minister in Easterhouse, it said of the Unit: 'This is an every-day tale of murdering folk, violence, venomous hatred, books, redemption, and hypocrisy.' The Unit had been voted a clergy-free zone by staff and inmates, but one regular visitor there – George Wilson – spoke persuasively to the prisoners to get Mr Ferguson inside. There he got to know Jimmy Boyle. 'What I discovered there was that there were powerful people who wanted him to fail, in order to prove their own theories that the likes of him could not change. One former Moderator was vehement that the Unit should be shut down forthwith. There were church people who – and I choose my words carefully – wanted him to re-offend.

'The sight of a notoriously violent man changing was strangely too much for some clerics.' He concluded: 'In my manse there is a special sculpture which is a symbol of hope. And there are desperate people in Easterhouse and in Barlinnie who have taught me more than theologians about the meaning of that most precious word, redemption.'

And that one word sums up the experiment. For all its successes the curtain still came down on the Nutcracker Suite. But you simply can't black out its historic role in changing people.

7

GANGBUSTER
AND A DICED CAP

Elliot Ness and the Untouchables are the mainstay of many a TV
and film drama about Chicago, a city like Glasgow with what the
police would call serious 'form' in the gangland stakes. But less
fêted, indeed perhaps forgotten by many, are Glasgow's own
Untouchables. The story of Sir Percy Sillitoe – the chief constable
who founded the Scottish division of the Untouchables, an elite
police squad, to battle with the gangs of the 1920s and '30s – is
one of the most fascinating in the *Herald* archives. Sillitoe led a
remarkable life spanning the Glasgow gangs, MI5, diamond giants
De Beers, and even the spy Guy Burgess. The tale began in 1931
when Sir Percy became Glasgow's chief constable, a position he
was to hold until 1943. He had learned his trade as gangbuster in
Sheffield and this experience no doubt led to his recruitment to a
city where pitched street-battles between gangs such as the Billy
Boys and the Norman Conks were a major problem.

But Sir Percy was an Englishman and it was said that many in
Glasgow were not happy about the appointment. In fact, the people
who should have been most unhappy about his arrival were the
men who swaggered the East End streets emboldened with their
weapons of choice: bicycle chains, open razors, hatchets, swords
and knuckle-dusters. They were about to meet their match in a
lawman harder than the toughest of the neds. A strict disciplinarian,
Sillitoe was known to his men as 'The Big Fellow' and 'The Captain'.

He formed his own Untouchables, a squad chosen for fearlessness and physical fitness, and set about teaching the gangs that from now on the rule of law applied in the city and no longer would they have the freedom to batter each other – or anyone who got in the way – to bits. This was no namby-pamby campaign, it was war on the neds using the only weapon the slum-dwelling warriors recognised – force. The reality of the Sillitoe technique is exemplified in a letter written to *The Herald* in 1992 by his son Anthony. Writing from London and commenting on a rash of newspaper stories at that time he said: 'My father . . . Gangbuster Sillitoe . . . would not be amused about a report about street warfare in Glasgow. He solved the problem years ago by enlisting tough cops, mainly Highlanders, to club first and then ask questions. I hope the present chief constable takes note.'

Such robust tactics might not be politically correct today but the fact is that Sillitoe and the Untouchables broke the gangs' grip on life in the deprived areas of the city. Further evidence of the physical nature of the 1930s police assault on the gangs comes from the obituary of William Smith, who ended up holding the top police job in Scotland, Her Majesty's Inspector of Constabulary. Smith was a university graduate born in Milngavie who was thwarted in his ambition to teach English by the lack of educational jobs in the depressed '30s. Ultimately he sought a second-choice job with the then Glasgow Police. Graduate policemen were a rarity in that era but it helped bring him to the attention of Percy Sillitoe. Young Smith boxed at welterweight for the police and was something of a fitness fanatic. All this encouraged Sillitoe to select him for the squad of young officers particularly selected to tackle the gangs. Typically Sillitoe wanted even more – so he sent Smith to Aldershot to train as a physical fitness instructor. This meant the young officer could test his abilities with criminals inside and out, for he also taught physical training to inmates in Barlinnie. Unlike Sillitoe who left the Glasgow force in 1943 to head MI5, William Smith went on to hold a series of top police jobs until his retirement in 1975. An interesting side-light to his career was that when chief constable of Aberdeen he started an underwater search team, something that had been pioneered in Glasgow when what was claimed to be the world's first such unit was formed.

But it would be wrong to simply categorise Percy Sillitoe as a gangbuster. He also waged war on graft within the old Glasgow Corporation. He proudly wrote about how a councillor was jailed and banned from standing for office for seven years for accepting a £10 bribe to enable a public-house licence to go through. And the underwater team apart, he innovated in many other ways, including the introduction of radio cars. In his battle against the gangs he used undercover intelligence to plot likely areas for fights and planned ambushes. He was clearly a man not to be meddled with lightly. During the trial in 1936 of Dr Buck Ruxton, the defence called in fingerprint experts from Scotland Yard to question evidence provided by Glasgow police. Ruxton had butchered his wife and maid and thrown the body-parts over a bridge near Moffat. This was the first time that prints had been taken from the dermis, or deep skin, as Ruxton had deliberately mutilated the fingers of the wife and housemaid. Sir Percy was unfazed. He sent the prints to the FBI who both confirmed the Glasgow team's conclusions and came up with damaging additional characteristics. Faced with the might of Glasgow's finest and the G-Men, the defence counsel Normal Birkett decided not to call the Scotland Yard witnesses; Ruxton was convicted and went to the gallows.

Another side of Sillitoe emerged in 1991 when wartime police reports were made public for the first time. Ironically for a man who was to become Director General of MI5, Sillitoe was openly opposed to compiling fortnightly intelligence reports for the Secretary of State for Scotland. He warned about the dangers of policemen asking questions for information that was to be the basis of confidential reports. Almost immediately on the outbreak of war he wrote to St Andrew's House, saying: 'There is a great danger that such a practice would be construed in the present circumstances as the beginning of the institution of a secret police organisation, of the kind from which the British people have always prided themselves they are free.' The response from the Government was to opine that – when it was considered desirable – the general public's reaction to the war should be assessed through 'discreet observations made by the police and reliable members of the Forces'.

In one of his reports the Chief Constable showed a powerful streak of social concern when he highlighted the fact that by October 1939 fully half the number of children evacuated from the city by the Government had returned to their homes. The fact that no schooling was provided for them was making parents so angry that they were petitioning local authorities to reopen the schools. According to 'The Big Fellow' many children, particularly in working-class areas, were running wild and greatly increasing the work of the police. All this was a long way from one of Sir Percy's late-life chores – working for the somewhat mysterious De Beers Consolidated Mines. He was recruited to set up an International Diamond Security Organisation to buy in the diamonds from an army of illicit diggers. This had some successes but then, as now, Sierra Leone was a major problem in the leakage of stones to unlicensed dealers undermining prices in the Dutch cutting centres.

Sir Percy also served as head of MI5 for a time, but he did not enjoy it. His son told a *Herald* reporter: 'My father died an unhappy man. By all accounts he was one of the most successful policemen in the country, but he hated his seven years as Head of MI5: he just detested the long-haired intellectuals who resented his sudden appearance.' His son also told of Sir Percy's fury when his then deputy Guy Liddell and Sir Roger Hollis – at that time heading to the top in the sister organisation MI6 – spoke over their heads in Latin. 'Let's get out of here,' he said to his son.

A remarkable footnote to the Sillitoe story is the revelation that at the end of his life, when he knew he was dying, he planned a bizarre visit to Moscow to confront spy Guy Burgess with the names of three people he was convinced were traitors. The instincts of the old policeman were surfacing in his final months. He was going to his grave with secrets of great treachery but he wanted the 'thief' to know that, although he had got away with the crime, the facts were known. But his wife forbade him, in no uncertain terms, to make the trip. And he died of leukaemia in 1962. His is a proud legacy in Glasgow's battle against crime. Sir Percy Sillitoe will never be forgotten when Glasgow and policing are discussed. But he had an influence on policing in more places than Glasgow. He introduced the chequered band to police hats, with Glasgow being the first to sport the black-and-white in this way. The style was soon adopted by all British forces and it even spread to Australia and Majorca.

8

OLD STONES AND NEW TECHNOLOGY

The change in the perception of Glasgow by its own citizens, as well as by the tourists who are coming in growing numbers, is remarkable. New Glasgow is a city to be proud of. And much of the physical regeneration is belatedly taking place on the banks of the Clyde. The Tall Ship, the 103-year-old Glenlee rescued from a rotting death in Spain, is now magnificently restored. Across the river the Science Centre and the futuristic Glasgow Tower dominate the waterside. More than £500 million is about to be spent on the Glasgow Harbour project on wasteland between the SECC and the Clyde tunnel – 2000 homes, two cinemas, bars and restaurants in a modern waterfront development. The Garden Festival of 1988 didn't immediately kick-start an architectural boom, but now, as the new century dawns, the riverfront is belatedly becoming the focus of regeneration. The halls of justice are playing a role. The new Sheriff Court, replacing a historic building in the Merchant City, is on the south bank; the recently refurbished High Court is on the north side, barely a Tiger Woods' drive away.

The Sheriff Court, something of a riverside landmark, is said by some to be the busiest court in Europe. It may face on to pleasant riverside gardens but inside, daily, the tawdry story of a city's criminal life is unfolded and exposed to justice. Across the river the North Court of the High Court is a place steeped in Scottish criminal history. Its £5 million facelift in 2000 was much needed.

Twenty-three years earlier the old court was badly damaged overnight during the trial of Walter Norval, whose exploits are recorded elsewhere in this book. A petrol-bomb lobbed through a window by criminals determined to stop the trial did extensive damage: until the latest renovation, traces of blackened wood caused by the fire were still evident. All that has been swept away along with the original dock and witness stands, but no amount of work by the most skilled carpenters and interior decorators can erase the memories of this foreboding place. The classical pillars of the impressive facade are said to be modelled on the Parthenon in Athens, and they face directly across the road to the entrance to Glasgow Green, now dominated by the powerful McLennan Arch. This structure was originally part of Robert Adam's Athenaeum in Ingram Street. When that building was demolished in 1796 the arch was saved and rebuilt at the foot of Charlotte Street. In recent years it was carefully taken down stone by stone and rebuilt facing the High Court as part of the plan to regenerate the riverside area. Nothing happens in Glasgow without a lot of carping and some writers on architecture believe it was better where it was!

But the story of the High Court is one of stronger stuff than disputes on aesthetics. Many grim dramas involving life and death have been played out in the wood-panelled rooms of the North and South Court. This was where Dr Pritchard heard that his fate was to die on the gallows just across the road. This was where the last man to hang in Barlinnie, young Tony Miller – a teenager who had mugged and murdered a gay man in Queen's Park – listened to the ultimate sentence being passed. Generations of Glaswegians on the way to their work places have watched as the famous blue Barlinnie bus – strangely sinister with its blacked-out windows letting outsiders catch a glimpse of the shadowy wretches inside – shuttled the accused and the convicted to and from the Bar-L. Those who left for Barlinnie after sentencing were heavy of heart. And none more so than those who had stood before Lord Carmont in the 1950s. Carmont helped curb the razor slashers with a policy of handing down lengthy sentences: indeed, anyone given a long stretch was said for years after to be 'doing a Carmont'. He died in 1965 aged 85. In those days newspaper headlines and layouts were more restrained than is the case now, but nonetheless Lord Carmont was remembered in the somewhat tabloid, for the *Herald*, headline on his obituary as the 'Judge who rocked Glasgow Underworld.' The accompanying photograph was of a saturnine figure in legal robes, an image that would not have looked out of place illustrating a Sherlock Holmes novel. Lord Carmont was a judge of the Court of Session and High Court of Justiciary for 31 years and was at work up to a fortnight before his death on holiday in Kirkcudbright.

An appreciation in *The Herald* opined that the paradox of John Carmont's judicial career was that he became best known as a judge to the man in the street in that branch of the law in which as a counsel he had little experience, and which as a judge he probably liked least. The writer went on to say: 'His salutary sentences on razor-slashers, knife-wielders and thugs in the Glasgow High Court in the years following the Second World War had a marked impact on the criminal classes and earned for him the respect and approval of law-abiding citizens.' Carmont may have been an outstanding authority on maritime and commercial law, but faced with a Glasgow hardman in the dock he was swift to send the villain down for a long period. Such salutary penalties were first imposed in 1952, when on one occasion he passed sentences of up to 10 years and totalling 52 years' imprisonment on eight people convicted of crimes of violence. This is the particular circuit that was said to have 'rocked the underworld'. *The Herald* went on to remark that '"copping a Carmont" became an established phrase in the jargon of the malefactors'. Yet it seems that the punitive sentences he imposed were not the reactions of a harsh judge. The appreciation praised John Carmont as the gentlest and kindliest of men, and said that the sentences were the logical outcome of his sense of priorities which demanded that the public were entitled to protection from the anti-social activities of the lawless. No matter the motivation, the tough sentences worked well with the city's neds quickly realising that they would face no mercy when in the dock in the High Court.

Carmont had a remarkable legal mind and his retentive memory was such that he was said to be able to quote, without reference to textbooks, a formidable number of decisions and authorities in both Scottish and English courts. He was also said to possess the ability to introduce a sense of humour into otherwise sombre proceedings. Once, when counsel was seeking a new trial in a damages action – alleging misdirection by the judge in that his charge to the jury was too brief – Lord Carmont reminded the court of an English case in which at the close of the trial, the judge turned to the jury and said, 'How much?' and no more. The man who wiped the smiles off the faces of Glasgow's toughest gangsters made a valuable, never-to-be-forgotten contribution to the city's fight against crime.

Long before Carmont had set about handing down his lengthy sentences, the tempestuous politics of the '20s and '30s had spilled over into the old High Court. Here the Red Clydesiders, led by John McLean, were prosecuted for leading political riots during the turbulent days of the Depression. And in much more modern times Scottish terrorism features, with several cases involving 'Tartan Army' activists. The troubles in Ireland sparked some top-security cases involving men accused of collecting arms for the UDA, UFV and the IRA. But the staple diet of the court was Glasgow's street villainy. Most of Scotland's major crime figures have walked through the echoing corridors of the High Court. Arthur Thompson, the Godfather of the Ponderosa, even managed to appear in the North and South Courts in one day. In one he was a witness in the trial of men accused of murdering his mother-in-law with a car bomb and then trying to kill him. The verdict was not guilty. Arthur then crossed the corridor to the South Court to appear in the dock himself. In the same court crime legend Paul Ferris was cleared of murdering Arthur 'Fat Boy' Thompson, the drug-baron son of the Godfather, who had been gunned down while on a weekend pass from prison. The panelled walls of this historic court were also the backdrop to mass murderer Peter Manuel's sensational sacking of his defence in 1958, a move that, however dramatic, did nothing to save him from the noose.

There is one certainty in the story of the High Court. No matter how many battles have been won in the fight against crime, the war will continue. Greed, jealousy, violence and wickedness will ensure that the cases that are heard behind that beautiful facade will fill the newspaper archives of the future. The lawyers dealing with them will, however, have a slightly easier time than their illustrious paper-shuffling predecessors. Now there are computers on the benches and judges will be able to access opinions and case histories via the internet. But the old stones still have their memories.

9

THE FACE A CITY
CAN NEVER FORGET

The Bible John murders in 1968 and 1969 provided the city with its most enduring mystery; indeed it is no exaggeration to say that the killings of Patricia Docker, Jemina McDonald and Helen Puttock are among the greatest of unsolved British crimes. Yet the face of the man believed to be responsible is recognisable to thousands of Glaswegians to this day.

Few Glaswegians who lived through the hunt for Bible John can forget the identikit image of the man suspected of the killings. This was Scotland's biggest murder hunt: more than 100 detectives worked on the case and 50,000 statements were taken. There were extensive door-to-door inquiries. Policemen travelled to military bases and boarded ships in the search for clues to the identity of the serial killer. Detectives spent night after night in the city dance-halls searching for clues and checking that the killer was not returning to the scene of the crimes. Massive resources were thrown into the manhunt. A Dutch psychic was consulted and enquiries were made as far afield as Hong Kong and Zambia. A thousand suspects were interviewed. Dental patients who had had their front teeth altered or replaced were traced and interviewed. At the time of the killing most men wore their hair long and around 500 barbers were interviewed in the search for a killer with short sandy hair. Bible John's penchant for smart suits led to hundreds of tailors being questioned. The possibility that the killer was mentally ill led to hospital checks. The notion that he had an interest in golf led to many golf clubs being visited by the cops. And for the first time in Scotland, widespread publicity was given to an artist's impression of the suspect drawn from witness statements. The technique of the photo-fit was just beginning to be developed at the time.

The three girls who died after a night at the dancing were 25-year-old Patricia Docker (killed in February 1968), 32-year-old Jemina McDonald (killed in August 1969) and 29-year-old Helen Puttock (killed in October 1969). After the second killing the police had sought help from Lennox Patterson of the Glasgow School of Art to draw a likeness of the suspect from descriptions given by witnesses. Jeannie – Helen Puttock's sister – first saw this properly at the city's Marine Police Office. She had had perhaps the best view of the man suspected of the killing: along with Helen, she had seen a wanted poster in Barrowland on the fateful night but had not paid much attention. But when she was shown a colour version of the poster in the city's Marine Police Office she was overwhelmed. She said: 'My whole inside just churned. To me the resemblance was there. When I looked at it, it's a funny feeling, it's like something just turns in your guts, you know, like a wee kind of shiver of something. When I saw that I thought, God, that's a terrific resemblance.' Lennox Patterson had produced an amazing image, lifelike and haunting. Now the detectives in charge of the case called him back to do a fresh drawing aided by Jeannie's description. Later she helped to compile the famous final identikit picture. Short hair, auburn or sandy in colour, dark eyes, crooked front teeth – these were the standard images, all repeated with remarkable regularity by witness after witness. The suspect was also consistently said to be politely spoken, immaculately dressed and always ready to quote the Bible. Few Glasgow folk can forget this artificially created impression of a killer. For months people looked at fellow travellers on the bus or the train; at cinema-goers or at dancers. And many thought they saw Bible John. One writer in the archives remarked that 'it seemed that half of Glasgow knew Bible John'. Helen Puttock's sister attended the astounding total of more than 300 identity parades. She also spent hours at factory gates, pubs and cinemas along with police handlers taking a secret peep at people fingered by the public.

One advertising executive of *The Herald* itself bore a passing resemblance to the man in the police portrait and had to be given a police letter explaining that he was not a serial killer. He was one of many Glaswegians unlucky enough to be in the same boat because of the features that nature had given them. In retrospect there is a humorous side to this, but at the time it was an ordeal to be looked at suspiciously by fellow citizens who seemed to be on some giant, failed collective murder-hunt. And no matter how accurate the poster, no matter how many had seen it, the identity of the killer remained a mystery. To this day the Bible John saga is a complex intermingling of many different strands, of clues and red herrings, a challenge to the most skilled criminologist.

The tragedy was played out against a backdrop of a city said to be 'dancing daft'. This was no exaggeration. In the 1930s the city had 159 registered dance-halls, though by the '50s this had dropped to around 100. At its peak, this translated into a figure of around 30,000 people going out 'jiggin' each night! Hundreds of thousands treasure their memories of nights at the Plaza, the Albert, the Locarno, the Dennistoun Palais, or the Majestic (the 'magic stick' of street patter). But perhaps the most legendary of all is the Barrowland. Founded by the McIver family, this dance hall was famous for bands such as Billy McGregor's and latterly George McGowan – though these days, restyled Barrowland is mostly a stop on the road-tours of the top bands and single artists. Perhaps a bit down-market from such as the Albert, it was nonetheless immensely popular – both with couples who were regulars, enjoying the sweet-and-low of swing bands oozing out the waltzes and foxtrots, and singles on the lookout for a melodious hour or two away from the factory or shop and the chance of a 'lumber' on the way home. Thursday, 'winching' night, was particularly popular with the over-25s. This was the arena in which Bible John stalked his prey.

The similarities between the three killings are remarkable, though there are some aspects of the cases that strike a discordant note. The three victims had all been raped. All had been strangled. Their bodies were found dumped close to their homes. All had been at the Barrowland the night before they died. All were known to have left the dancing with what was said to be a personable young man.

A fateful change of mind by the first victim, Patricia Docker, helped to seal her fate. On a cold winter's night she had left the Langside home she shared with her mother and young son, intending to spend the night at the Majestic ballroom. An auxiliary nurse at Mearnskirk, she was 25, pretty and a keen dancer. She decided that night to go to the Barrowland instead, a venue with its share of wide boys and ladies' men in those days. Her naked body was found the following morning in a lane near her family's home. Detectives swiftly found some especially disturbing aspects to the case. Pat Docker had been menstruating and a sanitary towel had been placed on her body. This was to prove a link with the other two killings.

The second victim, Jemina McDonald, was strangled 18 months later in August 1969. Mina McDonald was a single woman of 32 who lived in a room and kitchen in MacKeith Street. She had three children, the oldest 11, who were looked after by her sister if Mina wanted a night at the dancing. On the weekend of her death she went to the Barrowland on Thursday, Friday and Saturday. The reports said she was wearing a frilly white blouse, a black kimono-style dress, slingback high-heeled shoes and a pair of stocking tights. She had on a brown woollen coat and her hair was in curlers though she was probably wearing a headscarf. She carried a large leather-look handbag. Not long before midnight she was seen in the dance-hall in the company of a tall man with a well-cut suit and auburn hair. Later she was reportedly seen in London Road in the company of a man vaguely answering to the description of Bible John, and even later at 12.40 a.m. she was seen with a man on derelict property near her home. This was the last time she was seen alive. Jemina McDonald was found by her sister on the Monday morning, lying face-down on the floor in a condemned ground-floor flat in MacKeith Street. Her coat was half pulled off and her shoes were off. Her stocking tights had been removed and were torn. She had been strangled and punched in the face. Patricia Docker had also had face and head injuries, perhaps caused by kicking. Like Pat, Mina had been menstruating on the night of her death. The first victim was still wearing shoes though all of her other clothing had been taken off.

The third victim was Helen Puttock, a 29-year-old whose husband was in the forces and stationed in Germany. But he was home on leave in October 1969 when his wife suggested that she should go dancing to the Barrowland along with her sister. This sort of arrangement was not too unusual in the heyday of the dance-halls, and although there was a bit of a row, her husband reluctantly allowed her to go and baby-sat their two children. It was another night of entertainment that was to end in tragedy. But the Puttock killing had clear differences from the others. This time on the face of it the police had much more to go on; this time, there was a positive sighting of the killer. Helen and Jeannie had met a couple of men. Jeannie took to the floor with one of the men who was an excellent dancer and they spent most of the evening together. Helen, who was wearing a black dress and black shoes, seemed to have caught the eye of a neatly dressed man with well-styled hair who seemed to be a cut above the rest of the crowd in the Barrowland that evening – if not much of a dancer.

The sisters introduced their new friends to each other. It is no great surprise that both the men were called John, a name much in vogue in Glasgow dance-halls in those days when a married man often fancied a night on the town, taking off his wedding ring and putting on his sharpest suit. It is clear that Jeannie had plenty of opportunity to study Helen's John at close quarters. A further happening made the identification even more memorable. Jeannie was short-changed by a cigarette machine at the end of the evening and John took up her case for a refund with the manager and a bouncer. She remembers him being aggressive and confident with the air of a man who is used to being obeyed.

After this the four set off for a taxi rank but Jeannie's friend left to catch the late-night bus from George Square to Castlemilk. This man, who has never been traced, became known as Castlemilk John and like Jeannie had real insight into the mind of the killer. More of him later. The remaining threesome took a 20-minute taxi ride from Glasgow Cross to Scotstoun. Inside the dance-hall John, around 5'10" and aged 25-35, had been extremely polite but in the taxi he was said to be irritated. He had suggested that he see the two women home because after all, there had been two dance-hall murders. He seemed a charmer and the women obviously felt safe in his company. In the dance-hall and during the taxi journey he made several odd biblical references in passing conversation. When the taxi arrived at Earl Street John arranged for Jeannie to get out first and he continued with Helen who, it seemed, wanted to spend a little more time with her new 'friend'. The taxi was dismissed and no-one saw Helen alive again. But there was a sighting of a man answering to the description of Bible John on a late-night bus back from the Earl Street area. He was described as dishevelled with a red mark under one eye.

The next morning, a man taking his dog out for an early walk discovered the body of Helen Puttock. The attractive, lively brunette of the night before was lying face-down. Part of her torn clothing had been used to strangle her. There were abrasions to her jaw and the side of her head. Her nose and mouth had been bleeding and her purse with a few coins was missing. A gold chain she had been wearing was broken. A cheap cuff link was found on the scene and witnesses on the late-night bus said that the suspect had tucked a shirt-cuff into his jacket sleeve. But nothing left behind by the killer led to his identity being revealed. The detective in charge of the investigation was the legendary Glasgow cop Joe Beattie who died in 2000. The case involved him for more than 10 years until his retirement in 1976. The tireless dedication to the mystery by Detective Superintendent Beattie and another legendary Glasgow sleuth, Thomas Goodall, was often written about in the newspapers.

The key, at least to the killing of Helen, seemed to lie with Castlemilk John. And in 1993, when the *Evening Times* took another look at this vital link, Joe Beattie said: 'One of my biggest regrets is that Castlemilk John never came forward. That was a bad break in the investigation. He would have been able to help. He was in Bible John's company that night. And he may know something about the killer that would identify him.' The detective added: 'Bible John would have told the other man about himself. He might have said he was a member of a golf club. Or where he lived or worked, or what his hobbies were.' Joe Beattie had been criticised for relying too much on Jeannie's evidence and he says: 'I did rely on Jeannie a lot. And she was an excellent witness. But Castlemilk John may know things that Jeannie did not.' The police conducted extensive inquires in the Castlemilk scheme at the time, but to no avail. The *Evening Times* appeal also failed. Castlemilk John was not a suspect and is thought not to have come forward because his trips to the Barrowland were hidden from a wife or girlfriend. The files are still open. The work of hundreds of detectives – including Mr Beattie and Chief Inspector George Lloyd, Superintendent Tom Valentine, Detective Chief Superintendent Elphinstone Dalgleish and Superintendent Jimmy Bird – produced no result.

The identity of Bible John is still a mystery but there is no secret about how the alleged serial killer got his name. The man who gave the killer the tag that lives on in criminal history is *Evening Times* crime reporter John Quinn, who later in his career became perhaps Scotland's most respected writer on boxing. He tells the story himself: 'Why Bible John? Well, it was simply this. There seemed no more appropriate name for a man whose name was known to be John and whose calling-card of death was his fixation with the Bible and his habit of quoting from the pages of the good book. I did not do it – as was said later in some books on the subject – because of a flair for the dramatic. I meant it merely as the seemingly perfect tag to jog the memory of those whose paths may have crossed with the dapper dancer of death who made criminal history by being the first man to have an identikit picture issued with the approval of the Scottish Office.' John Quinn covered the killing and was told by 'Elphie' Dalgleish: "The man is thought to be called John and may speak of being of a family of two and having a sister. He may also speak of a strict upbringing and of a strict parental attitude to drink. The man may also speak of having a strict religious background and make references to the Bible."

'What more could a reporter ask?' wrote John Quinn. Bible John. It seemed so appropriate and the name was to make a stunning impact. After the briefing by Elphie Dalgleish, John Quinn literally ran to his newspaper's radio car. In those far-off days before laptops, mobiles and all the electronic paraphernalia of instant communication, reporters dictated their out-of-office stories to copytakers who listened to the calls on headphones and typed the literary gems down for the attention of the sub-editors. Generally a dedicated hack would phone his news editor before going on to 'copy'. John did just that as he said to the office, 'let's call him Bible John'. And the rest is history, as you might say!

But the book on Bible John is not closed. The case was back in the headlines in 1996 when the body of John McInnes was exhumed from a graveyard in Stonehouse, Lanarkshire. Twenty-seven years after the killings that had sent shivers of fear through dancing-daft Glasgow, a reassessment of the facts had produced a new theory. The belief that John McInnes was Bible John was not entirely new. He was one of the early suspects who fitted the description given by Helen Puttock's sister. He had been in the Barrowland the night before she was killed. And he had a military background which some of the detectives found significant. He was a sometime furniture salesman who committed suicide aged 41 in 1980. He was picked up and questioned within days of the Puttock killing but was eliminated from inquiries. There was certainly a superficial attraction to the theory that he was the killer, but one outstanding fact must not be forgotten: Helen Puttock's sister – the one person in the world apart from Castlemilk John who had seen the killer at close quarters – was convinced that he was not the man. She didn't pick him out at an identity parade and today remains certain that he was not the killer. Joe Beattie was not impressed either: at the time that the rumours of McInnes being involved resurfaced he was clear in his opinion – ten witnesses had had the chance to pick out McInnes and none did. Beattie said: 'If you have ten witnesses and they all say no, what do you do, do you haul the guy up?'

There were other details that went against any notion of McInnes as the killer. His clothes did not match those of the suspect and he lived nowhere near where the dishevelled man had got off the bus. But his name stayed on the files and on the case, with many others that were reviewed when the police began transferring files on to a computerised database. By now DNA tests had become a new weapon in the detectives' armoury. A small stain of semen found on the stockings recovered from Helen Puttock's body had been kept in a plastic bag in the event of a fresh investigation. And some of the modern breed of detective thought that a DNA investigation could solve the mystery. So, on a cold February day five years ago, the McInnes grave was opened. It was a grim scene. Once the frozen soil had been broken into, the body of McInnes' mother was removed (it had been laid to rest on top of his) and the suspect's remains taken for laboratory examination. The semen, kept all these years, failed to provide a match. After the Scottish test the samples were sent to Cambridge for further examination. Five months later they were declared negative and McInnes was officially cleared by the Crown – ending a long nightmare for his family, who had to endure local rumours even before the plan to exhume.

All sorts of other theories on the identity of Bible John crop up in the archives. Was the real killer the Yorkshire Ripper Peter Sutcliffe, in Scotland on a murderous spree? Was Bible John a seaman who visited Scotland on deadly visits months apart? Is he alive and living in England or abroad? The speculation is endless. But out of all the thousands of words written about this remarkable case, a handful stand out. Joe Beattie told *The Herald* before he died that he was never satisfied that one man killed all three women. And that is the final, unanswered question. Did Bible John exist?

10

THE MAN WHO RAN
TO THE GALLOWS

One minute past eight on the morning of Friday, 11 July 1958 is a moment of time etched forever in the minds of Glaswegians. I remember glancing at the kitchen clock and imagining the grim happenings in Barlinnie Prison that summer morning. It was a reaction mirrored by thousands of my fellow citizens.

This was the moment Glasgow rid itself of the menace that was Peter Manuel. But not his memory. It is strange, however, that Manuel and his evil deeds, though deeply locked into the city's collective subconscious, do not seem to have been given as much retrospective attention by the newspapers as his status as one of the world's most prolific murderers might suggest – though several books have been written about this most complex of criminals, a 32-year-old psychopath with a taste for killing for sexual gratification. It is almost as if the city has tried to erase the appalling memory of a hideous time by a conspiracy of silence. Perhaps the reason is that during the years of the killings, Glasgow and the surrounding areas lived through a nightmare of collective fear. The impact of a series of unsolved murders filling the papers day after day can't be underestimated: families wiped out and single women attacked, and no arrests – it was a troubled time when fear, suspicion and rumour were rife. It was said that in Glasgow and Lanarkshire it was almost impossible to buy door-chains or padlocks at the height of Manuel's rampage of rape, sexual assault, housebreaking and murder. The hardware stores enjoyed a bonanza.

Seldom has there been such a series of seemingly unlinked murders. For much of the time the police and the Press were sure of Manuel's involvement. But despite the intervention of many of the most fêted of the west of Scotland's top detectives, a combination of Manuel's cunning, some bad luck, and, it has to be said, some bad police mistakes, he stayed at large long enough to kill as many as 15 people. The policeman who is credited by some with much of the success of bringing him to justice was Chief Inspector William Muncie, a detective with a controversial career and a man who wrote in his memoirs: 'As I stood in the white-tiled cell at Hamilton police station and gazed at the killer of all those innocent people, I remembered how I used to go home in the early hours of the morning and quietly check the front windows and door.' Cynics might have remarked that some more checking of what Peter Manuel was up to might have been more worthwhile. To be fair, it was not one man against another – Mr Muncie was only one of a range of detectives involved in a massive investigation. Critics of police handling of the case make much of the fact that for at least five years, Manuel was well known to the authorities and suspected of much villainy but still managed to stay uncaged and kill innocent people. Muncie, known as 'The Boss', had a remarkable record of solving crimes in his patch. He believed he had a special intuition that led him to the guilty. But it took some time to apprehend Peter Manuel – though it must be said the Lanarkshire monster was a devious and clever man with a proven ability to deflect the most damaging accusations.

When Manuel eventually went on trial in May 1958, sensation followed sensation. It was a long-running saga; indeed in those days, more than 40 years ago, there was a danger that the mass murderer could have gone free. Until the late '90s the law insisted that a trial be completed within a 110-day period of the accused being committed to prison, and at one stage it was feared that the

Manuel trial – which lasted 16 days – could breach the time-limit, saving him from justice. But it was the defence team who sought an extension because of the complexities of the case and the trial went to a conclusion.

The saturation coverage saw reporters and criminologists from many parts of the world flock to Glasgow. Every last word of the trial was recorded in straightforward reportage, every nuance and possibility analysed by the specialists. It even made a bit of television history. The late Bill Knox, who was to become an extremely successful crime novelist later in his career, was hired to do twice-daily on-camera reports from the trial. He drove from the court to do lunchtime and evening round-ups on the evidence, the first time Scottish TV had reported in this way. The fact that the debate about the death penalty was arousing some public revulsion to the noose only added to the drama being played out in the High Court on the banks of the Clyde.

The special editions of the papers sold swiftly and crowds gathered outside the court daily, craning to see the arrival of the accused from Barlinnie and watch the coming and goings of the legions of lawyers and witnesses. In every home and every pub it was the topic of conversation. It is hard to believe nowadays how important evening newspapers were in letting the country know what was going on. Today, TV and radio are the prime sources of instant news, but back in the 1950s workers in factories and shops were isolated from what was happening in the world outside. The evening papers had huge sales outside the Clyde yards or at Singers' factory gate in Clydebank, where literally thousands poured out, hungry for news. Steelworks such as Ravenscraig in Lanarkshire were also important sales points, and the housewife in a scheme often depended on the evening paper for hard news. Indeed, one *Herald* veteran remembers working as a van boy in Dunfermline at the time of the Manuel trial. The circulation men were out on the streets of the housing schemes of Fife with thick special editions filled with the courtroom drama in Glasgow. They used what was known as the 'melody van' to attract attention and the miners and their wives flocked to buy. This was perhaps the high point for the evening newspapers, before the teatime television and radio news programmes forced them to become more entertaining and analytical rather than purveyors of hard news.

It seemed that the entire country was watching, in horrible fascination, the wordy conclusion to a story that had begun many years before in New York. Peter Manuel's Lanarkshire family had moved to America in an attempt to improve the life of both parents and children in the New World. Peter's father Samuel worked for a spell in a car factory in Detroit but it didn't work out. Peter Manuel breathed his first in the land of the free – actually in Manhattan – in 1927, but returned to Motherwell with his family in 1932. Scottish law ensures that at a trial the jury can view the evidence presented in court, for and against, with minds untainted by knowledge of the accused's previous convictions – or indeed any allegations made against him. A sound principle. In the case of Peter Manuel the jury were to remain unaware of a remarkable background that emerged to the police and other authorities long before the dark-haired, evil-looking Lanarkshire woodworker appeared in the dock accused of eight murders.

After their return to Scotland the Manuel family moved to Coventry, and it was here that Peter had his first brush with the law. Aged 12 he committed a second housebreaking while on probation for burglary and was sent to an approved school for three years. This was the start of a record that was to point to his ruthless disregard for the life of his victims and to a predilection for sex offences. He escaped from this establishment 11 times and when on the run stole to keep himself in cash. And even this early, the pattern of violence that ran through his life began to emerge. On one of his many burglaries he assaulted a homeowner savagely with a hammer. After the Coventry blitz the Manuels returned to Viewpark in Uddingston and young Peter joined them there after a spell in Borstal for robbing and indecently assaulting the wife of a school employee. It was clear that a life of crime lay ahead, though few could have imagined the scale of lawbreaking involved or that it would all end on the gallows in Barlinnie.

Three years after the Manuels' return to Lanarkshire, in March 1946, a woman who was walking home with her daughter was attacked on a deserted footpath between Mount Vernon Avenue and Carrick Drive in North Mount Vernon. Two other attacks in the same area followed. Four days later a nurse was attacked and the following night a third woman was attacked, beaten and raped. Manuel was taken into custody the next day and the three women were taken to an identity parade. Two of them picked out Manuel as their assailant. The third did not. But following the parades he was tried and found guilty. He had been on bail at the time of the attacks, facing charges of breaking into a bungalow. Forensic scientists had matched a heel-print found near the third attack with one of his shoes and he was convicted of this attack based on the forensic evidence. He was given a 12-month sentence on the first two charges when 14 similar offences were taken into account. The third, much more serious charge was dealt with by giving him eight years' imprisonment.

Strangely for a man with his background, it is said that he brooded in jail, didn't mingle with the other prisoners and, surprisingly, all the time claimed he was innocent. An extremely complex individual, Peter Manuel often exhibited Walter Mitty tendencies. In jail he boasted that his father was an American gangster who had died in the electric chair. At other times he claimed to have been involved with the British secret service. His pent-up anger was so strong that he attacked a prison officer in Peterhead and earned himself another year inside. When he was released he contacted a Lanarkshire police superintendent, accusing the police of framing him. These accusations were not taken seriously, and some say that this episode led to a desire to get revenge on the police, especially those in the area. He was to secure some satisfaction when pitting himself against authority in

July 1955. He was in the dock accused of yet another attack on a woman. He defended himself and won a verdict of Not Proven.

It was a short-lived success. In May 1958 he was in the dock in the High Court charged with eight killings: Anne Kneillands (17), Mrs Marion Watt (45), Vivienne Watt (16), Mrs Margaret Brown (42), Isabelle Cooke (17), Peter Smart (45), Mrs Doris Smart (42) and Michael Smart (10). The Cooke and Kneillands killings were classic Manuel attacks on vulnerable young women out on their own. The slaughter of the Watts, Mrs Brown and the Smart family were linked to break-ins, again a Manuel speciality. The trial was the culmination of a police hunt that had begun with the finding of the body of Anne Kneillands on a golf course in East Kilbride two years before, in January 1956. With Peter Manuel living not too far away and mindful of his record the police made him a suspect. But nothing came of their investigation and indeed, with the benefit of hindsight, there was much criticism of their efforts.

But before the actual trial more dramatic events were about to break around Manuel's head. In September 1956, when a Glasgow master baker William Watt was on a fishing holiday at Lochgilphead, the news broke that his wife, daughter and sister-in-law had all been slaughtered in the family bungalow in Burnside. Watt ended up in Barlinnie. The innocent victim of a series of coincidences, he was arrested and charged with the murder of his wife, his sister-in-law and his daughter who had all been shot at close range in their beds. The police believed at the time that Watt had driven from his hotel in Argyll back to Burnside to kill and returned to Lochgilphead to establish an alibi. There were all sorts of flaws in this theory. The timescale was wrong: taking into account the time of the journey – around two hours each way – and the fact that William Watt had breakfast in his holiday hotel around 8 a.m. while the victims were shot around 6 a.m., there was already a hole in the police case. Furthermore, there was confusion in reports that he had been seen driving around Loch Lomondside and that he was on the Renfrew ferry that night – the witnesses disagreed about the make of car they had allegedly seen him in. The car itself was supposed to have made a high-speed 200-mile journey in five hours but was seen at daybreak in Argyll covered in frost! Worse, by the time the witnesses went to an identification parade William Watt's photograph had appeared in the newspapers. It was a nonsense. Nonetheless, this innocent man spent 67 tortured days in Barlinnie accused of killing his family before the authorities faced facts, the farce ended and he was released. Strangely, when Mr Watt was in the Bar-L, the real killer – Peter Manuel – was incarcerated in a cell not far away, accused of housebreaking. Manuel, as already mentioned, had been a suspect in both the Watt and Anne Kneillands murders but there was too little supporting evidence in the view of the police.

William Watt had retained the services of Glasgow lawyer Laurence Dowdall and the legendary pleader received a letter from Manuel asking for a meeting to discuss the case. Astonishingly, at the subsequent meeting Manuel showed knowledge of the inside of the Watt home in Fennsbank Avenue, Burnside. He even let slip that Mrs Brown had been shot twice – something that Lawrence Dowdall did not know but which was confirmed by the police. The lawyer informed the police of the meetings and what Manuel had told him. The police did not react immediately by arresting Manuel, something that many commentators on the case found surprising. But after one wrongful arrest the police were perhaps over-cautious and may have felt that more evidence was needed before taking action. This was a tragic misjudgement, since with the killer at large another five people were to die before he faced a jury. William Watt met Peter Manuel on his release in 1957, and because of what transpired in their conversations he became more and more convinced that this was the man who killed his family.

Later that year Manuel is believed to have killed a Durham taxi-driver, Sydney Dunn. A pretty Mount Vernon teenager, Isabelle Cooke, was strangled; and at New Year Peter Smart, the manager of a civil engineering firm, was shot in his Uddingston home together with his wife and young son. Years of defending himself and of hoodwinking the police seemed to have given Manuel the notion that he was utterly secure. In an act of colossal stupidity he stole the Smarts' car and gave a policeman a lift into Glasgow in it. This, in conjunction with other acts of over-confidence and carelessness, led to his arrest. Then the man who – as many detectives had noted – loved to be in the limelight and the centre of attraction confessed to eight murders, including the slaughter in Burnside.

At last, on Monday, 12 May 1958, the trial of Peter Manuel began. In these days of lurid red-top tabloids, and the birth of what some cynics call the 'broadloid', it is interesting to note that the start of the trial only made an inside page of *The Herald*. The front page was still devoted to advertising, including the delights of the Tunnock's caramel wafer, a tasty bite produced in Manuel's Uddingston patch. *The Herald* noted that the indictment, which listed 228 productions and 280 witnesses, also alleged housebreaking as well as mass murder. Lord Cameron was the presiding judge, and Mr M G Gillies, advocate depute, was named to lead the prosecution for the Crown. The defence was led by Harald Leslie QC who later became Lord Birsay. Citations were issued to 60 potential jurors and accommodation for the chosen 15 reserved in a nearby hotel. The queue for public seats began to form at 7.40 on the Sunday night and by midnight it was around half a dozen, including two women from Edinburgh. The Press coverage was said to be unprecedented in Scottish legal history. Sixty-eight seats were reserved for reporters who had been issued with identity cards and tickets. These hacks were from the local papers, English titles, and the Commonwealth and foreign news agencies. A special bench nearly 20 feet long was built to cope with the productions and there was a bookcase for documents. A busy fortnight lay ahead!

The drama began swiftly. Manuel, described as an American-born woodworker, had just taken his seat in the dock between two uniformed constables when Harald Leslie QC rose to intimate a plea of not guilty and put forward a special defence. The full indictment was then read before the final jurors, six women and nine men. Manuel claimed that the Burnside murders were committed by William Watt, and that between the times the murders of the Smart family were said to have taken place he was in his home in Birkenshaw, Uddingston, with his family and others. The preliminaries were completed at 11 a.m., half an hour after the court had opened. The first of the long list of witnesses was a police constable from Lanarkshire. The early part of the trial was mostly concerned with the killing of Anne Kneillands, a crime to which Peter Manuel had confessed. But despite all the evidence produced in court it was ruled that the only source of evidence was the confession; there was no corroboration and in the end Lord Cameron told the jury to acquit Manuel on that particular charge. The situation in English law is different. Down south, a clear confession without any other evidence to support it has resulted in conviction.

Manuel had also confessed to killing Isabelle Cooke, but in this case there was supporting evidence – the confession included facts that only the killer could have known. Manuel was able to tell the police where her clothing would be found and that she had been strangled. He also indicated where the body could be found. The confession also played a role in the case of the Smart murders. He let the police know roughly where the gun used in the killings would be found and he knew details of the inside of the house where the horrific murders had taken place. The confession issue was dealt with in Manuel's appeal after conviction, when Lord Justice-General Clyde emphasised how essential it was in Scottish law that other evidence support the confession.

For most of the newspaper readers, the sensation of the trial was the decision of Manuel to sack Harald Leslie and conduct his own defence, and the appearance in court of William Watt. But before Watt himself appeared the jurors were regaled with details of Manuel's meetings with Laurence Dowdall and the police reaction (which seems, viewed from this distance, to be appallingly cavalier). Mr Dowdall told the court that while retained to defend William Watt, he had received a letter from Peter Manuel which he read out. The last paragraph said: 'I would like you to come and see me on Wednesday. The proposals I have outlined are to our mutual advantage, mainly due to the fact that I have some information for you concerning a recently acquired client of yours who has been described as an all-round athlete, Yours sincerely P Manuel.'

The meeting was arranged and at it Mr Dowdall said, 'What about Mr Watt?' He told the court that Manuel replied: 'Mr Watt is innocent.' Mr Dowdall said, 'How do you know?' His answer was, 'Because I know the man who did it.' 'If you know the man who did it, why don't you go to the police?' continued Mr Dowdall, and Manuel indicated in a few sentences that he regarded the police with some disapproval. There was laughter in court but it quickly ended when an usher shouted, 'Keep quiet'.

Mr Dowdall went on: 'I said, "what was the name of the man?" and he did not give me any. I said, "You had better tell me something about it" . . . Then he told me that on the night before the Watts – and I include Mrs Brown in that – were murdered a man had come to him and he had a gun in his possession, a revolver. He wanted Mr Manuel to go with him on a house-breaking expedition in Burnside. Mr Manuel told me he would not go and did not go with him. He then said he read about the murders in the papers and the man came back to see him. This man he described as being "in the horrors".' The lawyer went on with more detail of the conversation, but eventually said he had put it to Manuel that his story was very interesting but suggested that he might be indulging in a bit of leg-pulling. Manuel assured him he was not and the lawyer asked him to prove that the story was true, to which Manuel replied that he could provide some information about the Watt household. This he did. Mr Dowdall went on to say that he himself left the prison and went on to phone the police. Laurence Dowdall wanted to see the inside of the Watt house and this was arranged. The indications were that Manuel's knowledge of the house was accurate.

The court was told of further meetings with Manuel. Mr Dowdall continued to press Manuel to tell the police what he knew about the case, but he would have none of it. Manuel wanted to meet William Watt and a meeting was arranged. Laurence Dowdall told the court that after his third meeting with Manuel he went to the police, but before doing so he asked Manuel: 'What shall you do if I go to the police?' The answer was, 'I shall deny that I said it.' At the end of this evidence the judge, with some degree of understatement, said that the next witness might take some time and that he was not presently available. The court adjourned until 10 a.m. the next day, when the man in the witness box would be William Watt himself – the man Peter Manuel was accusing of the Burnside murders.

The first appearance of William Watt as a witness was a remarkable courtroom confrontation, a face-to-face between the two men. The drama was heightened by the fact that the master baker had to give his evidence from a wheelchair after being injured in an accident before the start of the trial. Towards the end of the trial, after Manuel had sacked his counsel, he was to demand the return to the witness box of Watt – another cruel turn of the screw on an innocent man. However, their first joust in court had jurors spellbound.

Questioned by the defence, Mr Watt told of the remarkable series of coincidences that had sent him to Barlinnie accused of murder. On the Sunday before the murders Mr Watt told of getting his car fixed in a local garage, something that was to lead to accusations that he was getting it ready for a swift drive to Burnside and back. He then went back to his hotel in Cairnbaan, planning a fishing expedition on the Monday morning. After dinner he went to bed and pared a corn to ease some pain he was suffering. This mundane act left a dab of blood on his bedsheets, something else to be used against him.

He then told the court of how he had been told of the murders while out fishing. The hotel had been informed by the police of the happenings in Fennsbank Avenue and sent someone out to the pool where William Watt was fishing to tell him that 'something had happened' and he should phone the hotel. At first he couldn't seem to take in what had happened and phoned his brother in Glasgow for more information. At this point in his testimony Watt broke down and sobbed for several minutes and was given water by court attendants. A doctor also stood by.

He recovered and looking at Lord Cameron remarked, 'I am sorry, my Lord'. The defence continued its questioning and Watt made a remark of some significance. He said that he had asked the police for a driver to take him to Burnside and that 'on the way down I was able to make myself contained. I made up my mind that this was done and breaking up would not do me any good whatsoever. I would go to the police and help them get the fellow who had done this terrible deed.' In fact, Watt's seemingly calm attitude in the middle of such great personal tragedy had helped form the opinion of some of the original investigators that he was involved. The evidence of the witness box on that Friday in May showed otherwise. William Watt was in the witness box a tiring two hours and his grilling by the defence was wide-ranging. His meeting with Manuel was raised, as was the business of his alleged identification on the Renfrew Ferry and Loch Lomondside. The state of his marriage and his finances were probed – the total insurance on his wife's life was a mere £50 or £60. But when the Glasgow baker described Manuel's accusations as a 'lot of nonsense' the jury believed him.

The trial next moved to the murders of Isabelle Cooke and the Smarts, with some moving moments when Isabelle's parents had to identify clothing belonging to their dead daughter. There were witnesses to Manuel being near the scene of the crime and other evidence that left judge and jury in little doubt as to the accused's guilt. Likewise his plea of alibi using the members of his family in the case of the Smart killings cut little ice. His confession played a role in these charges as well.

The real sensation in the closing days of the trial was Manuel's sacking of Harald Leslie QC. According to *The Herald*, the first hint of this 'unexpected development . . . came on the morning of the ninth day of the trial almost as soon as the court sat'. Famous Glasgow detective Tom Goodall was about to be examined by the advocate-depute Mr M G Gillies for the prosecution, when the prisoner stood up. 'My Lord,' he said, 'before the examination of this present witness I would like to confer with my counsel.' There was a moment of silence, then Harald Leslie told the judge, 'I think it would probably be desirable.' The jury were asked to withdraw, Lord Cameron went to his chambers and Manuel to the cells. Manuel talked to his lawyers for about a quarter of an hour and they eventually went on to talk to the judge in private. When the court reassembled after 40 minutes Manuel was carrying a file of papers which he placed on his knee. Beside him was a blue notebook he had used during the trial. In a moment almost unparalleled in the history of crime a mass murderer was about to embark on his own defence in an effort to avoid the noose.

Harald Leslie rose to his feet, and in a quiet voice which did not carry beyond the front row of the Press benches said: 'I have to inform your Lordship I am no longer in a position with my colleagues to continue in the case and that the panel is desirous of conducting the remainder of the trial. Unless I can be of further assistance, or my colleagues, I would accordingly withdraw.' Lord Cameron turned to the prisoner. 'Manuel,' he said, 'do you now wish to conduct your own defence for the remainder of the case, or would you like an adjournment to allow you to appoint another counsel?' There was no doubt in the arrogant, self-confident mind of the killer. He was now in charge of the defence, though he retained a couple of solicitors – John Ferns and Ian Docherty – for advice. He could make a lot of mischief with his old enemies, the police. He was centre-stage.

Manuel immediately started off by questioning various police witnesses, and his knowledge of the way the police worked, garnered over his criminal years, helped him to make some effective points (though it is clear with hindsight that even at this stage in the trial, the detailed case painstakingly built up against him by the police – together with his confessions – would lead to a conviction). Then he wanted William Watt recalled to the witness box. Perhaps the chance to question Watt face-to-face was one of his motivations in sacking his defence. In any case, although the judge restricted the re-examination of the Glasgow baker to certain points, he was brought back into court again in his wheelchair. The two men were only six feet apart and the archives report that after some preliminary exchanges Manuel put a series of short, direct questions to Mr Watt. At one stage Watt was asked if it was not the case that he had said it would have required very little to turn the gun on himself after he had shot his daughter. It looked as if the witness was about to break down and the judge told him to reply with either an affirmative or a negative. Mr Watt replied loudly, 'No!' and he went on to dismiss Manuel's accusations as lies and nonsense. No doubt in a reference to the Loch Lomondside accusations, Manuel even claimed that Watt had told him he was a better driver than Stirling Moss! More lies. When the cross-examination was over, Manuel – who observed the legal niceties, calling the judge 'your Lordship' and giving the witnesses the dignity of 'Mr' – said, 'That is all, Mr Watt, thank you.' Mr Watt was wheeled backwards out of the court gazing intently at his accuser. As he passed the Press benches his expression relaxed and he smiled at the reporters who had followed his ordeal and who knew him well.

The Manuel style of interrogation was direct. He asked one detective outright whether or not he was sure that he had killed

Isabelle Cooke, and got the unhelpful answer: 'I have no doubt whatsoever.' Nor did the jury. The 16-day trial was drawing to a close, but before the verdict Manuel had one last chance to save his neck, addressing the jury for more than three hours. Before that the prosecution presented a devastating summing-up of the evidence against him. The Watt accusations were blown apart particularly on the grounds of complete lack of motive and the candour of Mr Watt in the box. It was pointed out to the jury how improbable it was that a car that had supposedly been driven around 200 miles at high speed between 2 a.m. and 7 a.m. should be seen covered in hoar-frost at breakfast time. And the Webley revolver used in the killing was found in the Clyde at a point shown to the police by Manuel. Similarly his claims of alibi in the case of the Smart killings, and claims that his family had been threatened by the police, were disregarded. He had also shown the police where the body of Isabelle Cooke had been buried.

In his charge to the jury immediately following Manuel's final defence speech Lord Cameron said: 'For the past 14 days you have been listening to evidence which has covered a catalogue of crime that in gravity is certainly without precedent in this country for very many years indeed. And there is one unusual feature in this case which is possibly unique in trials for murder in our courts in Scotland, in that the accused himself has elected, some distance through the trial, to conduct his own defence.' He pointed out that the decision to defend himself had denied Manuel the distinguished forensic abilities and technical skill of the counsel who had earlier appeared on his behalf, and this meant that the jury needed to scrutinise the evidence to see that all points which could properly be made in favour of the accused were given due weight. He then paid tribute to Manuel, saying: 'I should add this – that from what we have heard in the past days and particularly today, the accused has presented his own defence with a skill that is quite remarkable.'

However cleverly he had presented his own case, Manuel could not move the jurors to consider him innocent of seven of the eight murders. Indeed his final plea seems, at this remove, rather lame for a man with his record of violence. He closed his address to the jury saying: 'I can only say that I have not murdered any of these people. I have got no reason to murder any of these people.' The jury retired at 2.24 p.m. and returned at 4.45 p.m. During this time crowds milled in the halls of the courthouse, among them magistrates and councillors, some wearing the traditional lapel flowers they received at the fortnightly meeting of Glasgow Corporation. The place was alive with the buzz of conversations and speculation about the outcome between visiting dignitaries, senior police officials and newspapermen.

The jury had been absent for about an hour when a buzzer was heard. The reporters scrambled to retake their seats. The tension was high but a uniformed court attendant appeared to announce that the call was not intended for the resumption of the hearing. The wait went on. At 4.45 – two hours and 21 minutes after the jury had retired – a bell sounded and this time it was an unmistakable call to return to court. Every seat was occupied and people in the overflow stood beside uniformed policemen on duty at the entrance doors. Peter Manuel was brought in by his escort, and during the few moments that elapsed before Lord Cameron entered he chatted amiably with a police officer. Sitting in a relaxed position with one knee raised and clasped between his hands he showed the composure which had been so characteristic of him during the trial. Moments later the verdicts came one by one. As the judge had directed he was declared not guilty of the Anne Kneillands murder. But there was a guilty verdict on all the other capital charges. One of the minor charges of breaking-in was found not proven and on another he was found guilty by a majority. Significantly, the jury was unanimous on the Watt killings, the killing of Isabelle Cooke, and the slaughter of the Smarts.

There was only one sentence. Lord Cameron was one of the country's most stern and tough criminal judges, but when he donned the black cap to pronounce sentence of death by hanging

Behind the grim walls of Barlinnie many paid the ultimate penalty for their crimes – a ritualised death at the hands of the hangman. Here the hardest of Glasgow's hard men, those spared the walk to the scaffold, spent years caged in cells in vile conditions.

Arthur Thompson went to his grave proclaiming that he was a retired businessman. In reality he was perhaps the most feared Godfather the city has seen. At one time his empire controlled most of the villainy in the East End and Arthur himself survived three gangland assassination attempts. ▶

◀ The hard man who reformed. Jimmy Boyle went from killer to celebrity sculptor, wine expert, Rolls Royce owner and the good life via Peterhead and the Barlinnie Special Unit.

◀ Hugh Collins was another who found the course of his life changed by a spell in the Nutcracker Suite, as the Special Unit was sometimes known. He became a respected writer but was often at odds with Jimmy Boyle.

Patricia Docker, Helen Puttock and Mima McDonald – the victims of serial killer Bible John. A night out in the bright lights of the dancing in Barrowland led to death.

Barrowland – where 'dancin daft' Glaswegians loved to spend an evening fox-trotting to the latest tunes. Behind the unimposing exterior lay a spangled world of sequins, spotlights and the throb of a big band and the chance of a 'lumber' – Glasgow patois for a date. For three girls, that choice backfired. ▲

◀ John McInnes was suspected of being Bible John and in 1996 his body was exhumed for DNA testing. But all the testing did was to add to the mystery. It cleared him completely.

◀ Joe Beattie (second left), a pivotal figure in the hunt for Bible John, talks to fellow detectives under a Bible John poster, one of thousands which flooded the city.

A face familiar to hundreds of thousands of Glaswegians – the famous poster image of the man named Bible John. The deaths of his victims held much of the city in fear for years.

Mug shots of 'Gentle' Johnny Ramensky issued in 1952, the time of one of his many prison escapes. The legendary safe-breaker worked for the secret service during the war but, come peacetime, he reverted to his previous life of crime. ▲

Sir Percy Sillitoe, a hard man known to his officers as 'the Captain', had a spectacular career as chief constable, leading his elite squad of policemen to victory over the pre-war gangs. ▼

The Special Unit was a ground-breaking penal experiment in Barlinnie. It turned around the life of many famous career criminals, who emerged to become decent members of society, but the Unit had many critics. This 1981 photograph gives a flavour of the unit where there were some of the comforts of home and the prisoners were treated as human beings.

The entertainer Frankie Vaughn came to Glasgow and, seeing the deprivation of schemes like Easterhouse, decided to do something about it. Along with like-minded locals, he became involved in the Easterhouse Project with the idea of getting the kids off the streets and giving them something to do. Here, in 1971, he is surrounded by young admirers at an event in the local pool. ▲

Perhaps the most famous of Glasgow's legendary defence lawyers, Laurence Dowdall. His dress was as sharp as his mind and for years he was the lawyer of choice for Glasgow's name criminals. Witty as well as cunning, he often brought laughter to court in a long and successful career. It was jokingly said that, when Rudolph Hess was arrested in Eaglesham, his first words were, 'Get me Dowdall!' ▲

◄ Joseph Beltrami's name is forever linked with that of Paddy Meehan. The lawyer's struggle for Meehan and his subsequent feud with his client filled many newspaper columns. The Great Defender, as he was known, was at the centre of many of Glasgow's most intriguing cases.

◄ Glasgow's courts attract controversial and outspoken lawyers and Donald Findlay QC is the latest in a long line. He is famous for his love of Glasgow Rangers and a series of spectacularly successful defences of clients on murder charges.

Mass murderer Peter Manuel was considered by many of the policemen who hunted him to be the most evil man they ever encountered. But it all ended on the gallows in Barlinnie and it is said that Peter Manuel almost ran up the final steps to the noose.

May 1958 and crowds gather under a summer sky to wait for the verdict on a trial that had held the city in its grip. The world's press churned out thousands upon thousands of words on Manuel, who was so confident in his own abilities that he had sacked his lawyer and defended himself. ▲

◄ A happy family snap – but Mrs Marion Watt and her daughter Vivienne were to die at the hands of Peter Manuel.

William Watt, who had languished in Barlinnie wrongly accused of killing his own family, is carried into the High Court on a stretcher after a pre-trial accident. The master baker from Burnside had the satisfaction of seeing the real killer of his family convicted. But in the witness box he had to endure cross-examination by Manuel himself. ▶

The interest in the trial of Peter Manuel was intense. The whole city followed the happenings in the High Court almost to the exclusion of anything else. Everyday the crowds turned up to crane over the railings for a glimpse of the accused or to watch the coming and goings of witnesses, lawyers and the police.

Three of the many detectives involed in the tracking down of Manuel – William Muncie, Tom Goodall and Alex Brown.

Isabelle Cooke, the pretty young Mount Vernon teenager who was strangled by Manuel.

TC Campbell and Joseph Steele were jailed for the Ice-Cream War murders but from the day of their trial they have proclaimed their innocence and fought for freedom through the Appeal Courts.

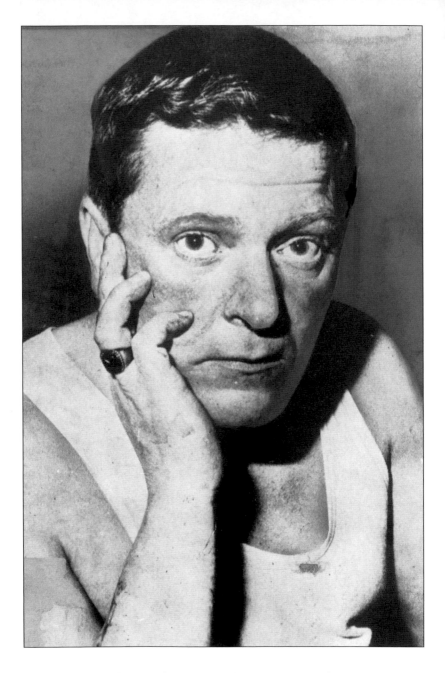

Paddy Meehan, a small-time crook who ended up doing seven years in solitary in Peterhead for a murder he did not commit. Freed after a high-profile campaign led by Joseph Beltrami and Ludovic Kennedy, he ended up in a feud with Beltrami.

The Ross bungalow in Ayr, scene of the horrific death of Rachael Ross who lay battered, bludgeoned and tied up for hours before dying.

◄ A letter from jail got the famous journalist and campaigner against wrongful convictions Ludovic Kennedy involved in the free Meehan campaign.

The Rochdale gunman James Griffiths, shot down by the police after an armed rampage through the streets of Glasgow.

◄ Nicholas Fairbairn, who defended Paddy Meehan in the original trial.

Jazzy tie, smart suit, white shirt, baby face – Paul Ferris on the steps of the High Court after being cleared of murdering Arthur 'Fat Boy' Thompson Jnr. But a few years later the smirk was gone and Ferris was sent down at the Old Bailey for gunrunning.

Bobby Glover (above left) and Joe 'Bananas' Hanlon, two East-End hard men, made a spectacular exit from the scene when they were found dead in a car on the very morning of Arthur Thompson Jnr's funeral. It was a real Mafia-style touch.

Manacled and surrounded by police, Arthur Thompson Jnr – a wannabe hard man in the view of most of the East End – is led away in suit, collar and tie to start a drugs sentence. The man who was to die in a hail of assassin's bullets never gained the respect of gangland.

'The Hammer' and some of his men – Chief Constable Sir David McNee, with some of the recipients of Long Service and Good Conduct medals in 1977. These are men who battled day in and day out on the streets of Glasgow to rid the city of its unenviable reputation for crime.

Leaders of the 'thin blue line' down the years on Clydeside: (from the top left) Sir James Robertson, Sir Leslie Sharp, Sir Andrew Sloan, Sir John Orr and Willie Rae.

he was said by some reporters to have been 'visibly moved'.

Predictably, taking into account his opinion of himself as a match for any policeman or lawyer, Manuel appealed. Among his many grounds he claimed that 'the alleged confessions both written and verbal should not have been submitted as evidence' and he claimed misdirection of the jury by the judge. Lord Clyde, Lord Carmont and Lord Sorn dismissed the appeal. After this Manuel confessed to other murders and it seems certain he killed between 12 and 15 people. On 9 July any hope he might have had of dodging the noose disappeared when he was woken in his cell in Barlinnie and told that the Crown saw no grounds for a reprieve. The news was given to him in the condemned cell by Bailie Blas, who travelled to the prison with the town clerk depute Joseph C Dickson. Bailie Blas undertook this duty in the absence of Lord Provost Myer Galpern, who was on holiday.

Considering the high profile of the case, it is surprising that only 12 people were outside the prison at one minute after 8 a.m. as the monster went to his death. The first official indication that the execution had been carried out came at 8.50, by which time a crowd of around 30 had assembled, when Bailies John Paterson and John Macdougal left the prison. Asked if Manuel had said anything before his execution Bailie Paterson said 'no' and Bailie Macdougal said, 'he made no reference to anything'. The two Bailies said the hanging was carried out in a satisfactory and expeditious manner. Later it was claimed that Manuel ran the final steps to the scaffold. The game was finally up.

There was an intriguing postscript to the Manuel saga in 1995 when secret papers relating to the case were revealed. They showed that there were doubts about his sanity held at the highest levels in Government. The Secretary of State and the Lord Advocate were so fearful of public criticism if Manuel had been reprieved on the grounds of insanity that they made plans to brief a sheriff and invoke a disused legal power in an attempt to deflect criticism if this had happened. From the released papers it emerged that shortly before his appeal was to be heard, Manuel began to manifest signs of madness that the authorities believed to be feigned. All this a few weeks before his date with the noose. An element of panic seemed to grip senior Government ministers, law officers and civil servants. The prospect of the mass murderer escaping justice by being declared insane appalled them. Manuel had been examined by three psychiatrists before the trial and one of them had described him as having 'psychopathic' tendencies. A Royal Commission into the death penalty had advised that the courts should take more account of psychopathic behaviour when considering execution.

These 1995 documents, released 20 years early under an Open Government initiative, said that the Home Office and the Lord Advocate were awaiting further medical reports. The medical reports revealed that a mere four days before his appeal was to be heard, and shortly before a meeting with his solicitor, Manuel was found on his prison bed frothing at the mouth. This led to his stomach being pumped but nothing was found to explain it. The killer simply refused to communicate with anyone. Two medical commissioners who tried to interview him reported that he was faking madness, saying: 'We consider the symptoms he is presently displaying are consciously motivated.' There was also the suspicion that Manuel may have gained knowledge of mental illness from his sister who was a nurse in mental institutions. The released file told how Manuel, while being examined, sat huddled in a chair, grimacing, pouting his lips, shrugging his shoulders, clutching his stomach and moving his head from side to side.

But in the final medical report it was concluded that Manuel was well aware of the possibility of saving his neck by being declared insane. It was said that 'it was well within his capacity to produce a convincing and suitable display of mental disorder' if it was of use to him. The documents also revealed that a last-minute plea by his mother to have him examined by an independent psychiatrist was rejected by the Scottish Office.

11

'GET ME DOWDALL' —
THE DEFENDER AND OTHER
HIGH-FLYING LEGAL EAGLES

For many years in Glasgow, whenever the cops felt a villain's collar, the arrested man would almost certainly utter the words that have earned an unforgettable place in Glasgow's criminal history: 'Get me Dowdall.' Laurence Dowdall, the legendary 'pleader's pleader', was the defence lawyer of choice for anyone facing a stretch in the Bar-L. As a young newspaperman in the '50s it was impossible not to be aware of his legendary dominance in the courtroom. And he was one of a line. He was followed by Joe Beltrami, aka 'the Defender' or 'the Sage of West Nile Street', Ross Harper and today Donald Findlay QC as number one in the public perception of the foxy, often witty and skilled defence lawyer. In Glasgow there was always plenty of work to be done by such men!

This book has looked at the part in the city's history played by untold numbers of hard men – both the razor merchants, armed gangsters and extortionists, and the equally tough beat policemen, detectives and chief constables who took them on. In this grim battle the defence lawyers played a vital role. Often they used their great skills to 'defend the indefensible', as the layman might see it. They gave of their best to help knifemen, rapists, muggers, godfathers, gangsters and drug-dealers escape the sentences their crimes deserved. They used their flamboyance and forensic skills to spectacular effect. They made money in large dollops and lurid headlines day by day.

But no matter the public perception of these men and the many others like them who slogged in the courts, they played a vital, if complex, role in the overall battle for justice. An article in the archives by Austin Lafferty, a lawyer who has become a well-known writer and broadcaster on matters legal, made the point powerfully. He remarked on the show-business habit of concocting dramas like Rumpole of the Bailey and Perry Mason in which the lawyer is a starry-eyed defender of the hero who is, of course, wrongly accused. Fine, but what the man in the street inevitably asks is, how can you defend someone you know to be guilty? Austin Lafferty writes: 'The whole world, even the bit populated by quite intelligent people, sees lawyers as skilled in lies and smokescreens, with no other aim than the acquittal of even the most criminal of accused persons.

'As ever, the legal profession does little or nothing to inform the public which it serves and protects. And the first thing it should do is at least to proclaim that it does actually serve society as a whole and not just one client to the exclusion of all other interests and duties. Rumpole gives part of the explanation when he says that he is just an old legal taxi on the rank, ready to pick up the next fare, no matter how disagreeable. It is not the job of the defence lawyer to win at all costs. There are strongly held ethics, and often a balancing act between the interests of the client and of justice.'

He goes on to highlight the old Glasgow notion that 'Ye widnae be in the dock if ye werrnae guilty', and the assumption that it is perfectly obvious to anyone who reads the papers that the accused 'must have done it'. Austin Lafferty adds that the instinct to convict on media evidence is never far below the surface, no matter how responsible the reporting of the crime. 'It's often we see a baying mob outside a police station or court, when someone has not been convicted, but merely arrested or charged. The more sordid the crime the more vicious the reaction of the public. Never mind the evidence, get on with the trial. How can you defend the indefensible? Because the alternative is barbarism and the lynch mob.'

And there is no doubt that good defence ensures that the prosecution must do their job properly in proving the absolute guilt of the accused. The job of the defenders needs to be done, and few have done it more successfully – and on occasion as entertainingly – than that master of the jury trial, Laurence Dowdall. Jack House, legendary observer of the Glasgow scene, often referred to him as 'Glasgow's answer to Perry Mason'. But maybe if we take into account a tribute from Sheriff Len Lovat, Jack should have been telling the world that Perry Mason was Los Angeles' answer to Laurence Dowdall! Mr Lovat once remarked: 'Anyone speaking at the same platform, or table, or court as Dowdall would pale into insignificance. There is just no-one to compare with him for wit, delivery and content.'

Dowdall was a truly remarkable man who at 86 returned from retirement, in 1992, to work as a consultant with his old firm, founded with his friend Joe Hughes almost 50 years before. But court appearances were now out. He told *The Herald* in a lengthy interview: 'I couldn't go into a court now because the judges are so much younger than I am and the sheriffs are just boys. You feel embarrassed about getting up and pleading at my age.' Despite his advancing years he was still pretty spry and was bemoaning the fact that he had had to take a taxi to work since his car was giving trouble. He told the interviewer that there was no legal background in the family and that it was the 'parry and thrust' of the courtroom that attracted him to the law as a career. He graduated with distinction from Glasgow University and recalled one of his early cases in which the fiscal, the defence (himself) and the accused all had degrees in law!

His role in the trial of Peter Manuel and the clearing of master baker William Watt of the murder of his family has already been described, but looking back on his career the old pleader recalled two interesting aspects of that famous case. In one of his many meetings with William Watt he asked him if he wanted to intimate any claim for damages for wrongful arrest. The baker replied: 'No, the police were just doing their best.' Laurence Dowdall had also been asked by Manuel's mother if he would defend her son, another indication of his reputation as the best defence around. Dowdall told her he couldn't do it, as he would be a witness for the prosecution. Mrs Manuel was a very devout woman, he said, and told the lawyer that if her son had done all these 'terrible' things she wished he would just confess and plead guilty. Mr Dowdall went on: 'I told her the only way he could be defended was by getting expert evidence to say that he was insane at the time and she said she would never agree to that. The funny thing was that his sister was a mental nurse and she was stoutly maintaining that he was all right.'

Another high-profile murder trial was that of James Robertson, a Glasgow policeman who was convicted in 1950 of killing his mistress by running her over with a car. He then reversed over her to make sure! 'That was a sad, sad case. The extraordinary thing about it was that if he had told the truth in the witness box he would never have been convicted. His wife knew well that he had been conducting this liaison but he said he was not going to let her down in public.

'If he had told the truth and admitted he had this illicit liaison with this woman McCluskey then he would have got off. The very first question the prosecution asked him was, "What was Miss McCluskey to you?" He replied: "A casual acquaintance." Prosecution counsel used this like a knife; and every time he mentioned the phrase "casual acquaintance" he turned the knife and it was dreadful to see.' Had they known of the relationship they may have viewed the killing in a different, more sympathetic light. There could even have been a lesser charge or sentence. But at the trial Robertson would only allow the jurors to see him as the cold-blooded killer of a 'casual acquaintance' rather than a man in a tortured relationship with wife and mistress.

Mr Dowdall added: 'Robertson was about 6' 2" and by the time counsel had finished with him he looked about 5' 2". He just would not admit he had been carrying on with this woman. I saw him three or four days before he was hanged and he asked me to thank Jock Cameron and Manuel Kissen (his defence team) for the work they had done. He thanked me and then he said: "I know I am going to hang in three or four days' time, but I am still glad I didn't let my wife down in public". It was extraordinary.' The Robertson case and his execution had a great effect on Laurence Dowdall, a man of much humanity. It also played a pivotal role in the career of Bill McVey, who climbed from trainee officer to the top of the tree in the Prison service. In 1991, as Deputy Director (Operations), he remembered when as a 25-year-old officer in Barlinnie he walked the 20 yards from the condemned cell to the Hanging Shed in Barlinnie with James Robertson. He stood to attention at the side of Robertson as hangman Albert Pierrepoint placed the noose round his neck and despatched the former policeman into eternity. As he left the spot Bill McVey vowed he would never again take part in such a grim ritual. He told the *Herald* man: 'It did not turn my stomach, but I remember feeling awful. It turned me against capital punishment for all times and I believe calls for the return of capital punishment are rubbish.' He pointed out that those who bray loudest for the return of the rope have no experience of it in practice.

Laurence Dowdall later learned from the prison padre that Robertson faced death with composure. And Bill McVey recalls that throughout the six-week death-watch the policeman held out no hope of a reprieve. He believes now that the state can no longer take human life without itself being branded a murderer. By a macabre coincidence, Joe Beltrami – who was to succeed Laurence Dowdall as the pre-eminent defender of his day – was watching the Robertson trial as a law student. He recollected the awful, fearful tension of the final minutes in the courtroom from guilty verdict to the judge putting on the black cap.

But there were many lighter moments in court. Dowdall always regarded humour as one of the most effective weapons in his armoury. 'A touch of humour is a great thing for a jury. Try to get the jury on your side, giving you a little smile or nod of encouragement. You don't bamboozle juries. Juries are sensible people. But if you can inject a sense of humour they approve of you. You encourage them to like you. Don't antagonise them. You can get their sympathy by cracking the odd joke. And once you get the jury on your side they are less likely to convict.'

The sense of fun was shared in those days. The great pleader remembered appearing just before the Second World War for a client who had the misfortune to be called Joe Stalin. He had been charged with breaking the blackout regulations. The sheriff asked the fiscal the value of the rouble to the pound. And the fiscal, who had not the faintest idea, voiced the opinion that it was on a par with the pound. 'Very well,' said the sheriff, 'I'll fine him five roubles.'

In the same piece Laurence recalled a humorous incident in an identity parade. He had a client with a limp and one day the police called him in to a parade. In those days the witness and the lawyer looked through a sort of peephole arrangement. All the people in the parade were roughly the same height and appearance, and a taxi-driver who was supposed to identify the guilty one was at a loss. He asked for them to walk and Laurence thought that he was sunk since his client's limp would give the game away. But he had not counted on the ingenuity of the men in the parade. On the order to march in a circle, some collusion had them all going round with the same limp!

Laurence's own quick-wittedness with juries was legendary. A *Herald* reporter remembers a case when a witness was trying to impress the court with his ability as a trained observer. Laurence suddenly turned his back on the witness and asked him to tell the court whether he (Laurence) had a moustache (which he did). It was a huge gamble which paid off, as the alleged trained observer could not answer with any certainty.

Maurice Smyth, another respected pleader, tells of the occasion Laurence Dowdall took a procurator-fiscal to task for calling a production in a trial 'a pair of knickers'. He floated the garment in the air and insisted that such a diaphanously, gossamer confection should be described as panties or scanties. Female undergarments seemed to feature frequently in courtroom banter. In another case, when a young man was charged with assault with intention to ravish, Laurence had guarded his most important production throughout the trial. With high drama he produced it at the critical moment, only to be deflated when the angry young woman involved announced that the flimsy undergarment was 'mothproof, fireproof and tearproof'.

Mr Smyth remembered another humorous occasion when 'he not only blew his own trumpet in court, but also blew up a condom – and with it the Crown case when he set it afloat and it dive-bombed the jury.' Everyone, it seems, has a Dowdall tale. One reader wrote of the time early in the great man's career when he was defending in the Marine Police Court in Partick. It was a no-win situation. A Glasgow landlady had been caught red-handed selling bottles of whisky intended for export at £5 a time. Having failed to dent the testimony, Laurence turned his attention to the 100-odd bottles of whisky that festooned trestles, tables and chairs in the courtroom. 'How,' he asked, 'can the police maintain there is whisky in all these sealed bottles without submitting them for expert analysis? They could all be filled with cold tea.' Amid hilarity the magistrate offered to test every bottle. Laurence capped the laughter by intoning that he could not 'submit his honour to such an onerous and time-consuming task'. The reader, one Donald McNicol from the West End, concluded his letter – Laurence Dowdall was a lawyer with a sense of humour and a trier for even the most hopeless case.

But it was not all laughter in court. The death of Laurence Dowdall in 1996 was both the end of an era and an occasion for his distinguished colleagues to pay their respects to a legal legend. Men of the law famous in their own right, like Len Murray, Tom Brannigan, Bill Dunlop and Joe Beltrami, were following in the footsteps of an original. Joe Beltrami worked with him on many major cases. And the Great Defender – as Joe became known – remembered: 'I never once failed to learn from him in court. He was a wonderful tactician in court and I tried to model myself tactically on him. What really impressed me from even those early days was his complete knowledge of every case. He knew his cases backwards; he had a goal in view from the outset, knew exactly where he was going and as often as not reached that goal.'

A tall and immaculate figure, he had a rich voice and always cut a fine figure in court, giving an impression of real gravitas. He had a great run of courtroom successes, but a retired sheriff's officer told me that the great man often tried to be careful to choose winnable cases. If the evidence was against his client he would advise a guilty plea and would then argue in mitigation. If the client insisted in pleading not guilty against all the evidence he would often walk away. Clearly, among his other attributes was a strong streak of realism. On his death his long-time friend Robert Cassidy said: 'Laurence defended his clients with great skill, humour and humanity but his reputation went further. The bench respected him – for his integrity, his great knowledge and also, importantly, for his brevity. He was listened to by judges with an interest in pursuing justice. One of his chief virtues as a lawyer was never to be long-winded or boring to the jury.'

Interestingly the word humour features strongly in tributes to the life of Laurence Dowdall. That attribute was also part of the success of the man who was to become Dowdall's natural successor as a legal household name, Joe Beltrami. Joe was of Swiss extraction and when he was a youngster his family were involved in perhaps the most famous chip shop in Glasgow, near Glasgow Cross. Joe was brought up in a flat in the Bridgegate along with his younger brother Ray, who was to become a highly respected award-winning photographer with the *Evening Times* before dying tragically young. Joe used to work in the chip shop for pocket money, and this upbringing is credited by one writer in the archive as being a major contribution to his success – as he has always retained the ability to communicate with people with similar backgrounds, on whatever side of the law. Joe himself says: 'I spoke the language of the people I was representing. I was brought up in the same places, I was not an outsider coming in from somewhere like Bearsden.' The man who was to become known as 'the Sage of West Nile Street' tells an intriguing tale of how he came to the law. A chance meeting was to change his life. Joe was on his way to matriculate on to an arts course at Glasgow University when he met an old school friend. 'I boarded the tram from home intending to matriculate MA, and I changed it to Bachelor of Law from the time the friend came on the tram car at Charing Cross to Gilmorehill.'

It was to be a wise choice: he was a natural pleader. After he qualified he set up in practice on his own in the mid-'50s – after having difficulty, as a Roman Catholic student of law, in finding a practice to take him on as an apprentice. It is reputed that his first fee was £5, all his client could afford. From such an inauspicious start Joe Beltrami went on to instruct in many murder trials, the names of his clients reading like a roll-call of Scotland's underworld. Perhaps the highlight of his career was helping to win a Royal Pardon for Paddy Meehan in 1976. Meehan had been wrongly jailed for life in 1969 for the murder of pensioner Rachael Ross during a break-in at her home in Ayr (this story is told in greater depth elsewhere in this book). Joe also wrote a book about the case, *A Deadly Innocence*, but it was just one of thousands that he was involved in. He was often the right-hand man of the flamboyant former Scottish Solicitor General Sir Nicholas Fairbairn in murder trials. Joe also used his nickname 'the Defender' for another book with the catchy subtitle of *Tales of the Suspected*!

Joe Beltrami was also linked in the public eye with Arthur

Thompson, with whom he had an 'excellent business relationship' for more than 30 years. The Glasgow police were in no doubt that Thompson Snr was a Godfather of Glasgow crime with tentacles spread into many an evil ploy. But the tag Godfather rankles with Joe Beltrami – the Great Defender didn't like it when Arthur Snr was alive, and he continued to dislike it after his death. He told one young reporter: 'I represented Arthur for many years. People always claimed that he was in charge of organised crime in Glasgow, but I never accepted that. Arthur used to scoff at the term Godfather and made a point of getting me to take action when the media used it. He was nothing like an organised crime boss in Chicago with a team of lieutenants and henchmen in structured form around him.' He went on: 'That was never the case with Arthur and it is not the case with any other person in Glasgow. There is no "El Supremo" or big city boss controlling things. I am not saying we do not have crime, because we have plenty of that. What you find is that Glasgow has people who grow up and surround themselves with like-minded people who get involved in crime.

'These people then carry out criminal acts. Is that organised? Well, one man has to organise holding up a bank with a gun before he does it, but I don't think anyone would call that organised crime. Organised crime, as defined by the National Criminal Defence Service, does not apply to what we have here. We have major problems with drugs but it is all small groups of people. There is no kingpin directing operations from an office in the city. In London and other major world cities, organised crime is the domain of Mafia-type groups. In Glasgow you may have tiny strands of this but it amounts to nothing. People always talk about Triad wars in the city, but how often do you read about Chinese people being attacked or going through the courts? It is not a major issue. I keep my eyes open to what is going on in this city all the time and I can say the whole thing is a fallacy.'

On one occasion Arthur Thompson showed his appreciation of

the Defender in a gift – a magnificent mahogany box which when opened was shown to contain 50 Havana cigars in three sizes, small, medium and large. Each was decorated with a tasteful red paper band on which the name Beltrami was printed. There was a humidor to control the temperature and ensure that Cuba's finest stayed in top condition, and a drawer containing a mysterious white powder. Joe investigated this odd substance with some suspicion but found that the powder was for dusting the fingers after smoking a cigar in order to remove the odour of finest tobacco. The donor of this magnificent gift was one Arthur Thompson, who at the time was having some legal difficulties resulting from the murder of his son. The cost of the gift was not revealed but as the late Damon Runyon might have written, it was certainly no small quantity of potatoes.

The use of the word Godfather is open to much interpretation and argument, but on the strict use of the words with reference to organised crime Joe got support for his views from Gerry Brown, past President of the Glasgow Bar Association. He told the same interviewer that: 'NCDS alleged that organised criminals in Britain were using lawyers, accountants and bankers to disguise their activities. This is almost impossible in Scotland because the system here is very strict. Solicitors are audited every two years by the Law Society and we have to identify the source of any cash.' Talking in August 2000, Mr Brown was of the opinion that Glasgow was not open to be used as a centre of organised crime in the strict definition of that term. And the police agreed. But there are Godfathers and Godfathers, and they live on in the public perception – as well as in the minds of many expert observers of the criminal scene.

However it is undeniable that when Arthur Thompson was alive Joe took on the media on his behalf. When Arthur went to war on an Edinburgh Sunday newspaper he had the assistance of both Joe Beltrami and another famous Glasgow lawyer, Martin Smith, a man who more normally tried to keep newspapermen out of the dock in his other role as a newspaper night lawyer. (Indeed, I remember with gratitude when Martin's firm and one of his then partners, Alastair Bonnington, managed to get me cleared when as a young journalist I ended up in the dock accused of publishing information that might prejudice a trial.) Martin and Joe shared an unusual legal distinction: Joe and his lawyer son once appeared together in the same trial; likewise Martin and his father Hugh. In this case Martin was the fiscal and his dad appeared for the defence in a shoplifting case, drafted in as an understudy for a colleague. *The Herald* asked Big Martin to tell them who had won the case. 'Who do you think? But it was a hard-fought duel' was the reply.

Joe enjoyed a hard-fought duel. And he never held back. A colleague described his approach as having the subtlety of a Sherman tank going over a tray of crystal. A good example of his style was the tale of a Beltrami client who had been arrested at 10 p.m. but not charged till 4 a.m. The Defender claimed that this smacked of the Russian system where people could be detained for years without charge. He thundered to the jury: 'Your choice is between my client and the Rutherglen police who practise the Russian system.' The verdict was not guilty.

And Joe could tell a tale against himself. There is an amusing anecdote in the files when he talked about a lesson learned in court in his early years. 'It is a well-known axiom that the good lawyer does not ask questions of the prosecution witnesses unless he knows, or has a good idea of, the answer he will receive. In the '50s I remember defending a client charged with wilful fire-raising. The premises in question were the Berger paint factory in Glasgow where my client worked until he was sacked.

'The crime took place in the late evening when the lighting in the street was not of the best. Two young CID officers claimed in evidence they had recognised my client at the front door of the premises before he escaped. While cross-examining one of the officers, I made the point that it was dark, the street lighting was inadequate, and the nearest the witness had been to the disappearing figure was all of 150 yards. I went on to suggest it would have been extremely difficult to make an accurate identification in those circumstances.

'The officer agreed. I then asked him what sort of eyesight he had to have to achieve such accuracy. His reply was deadly: "20/20. I was a night pilot with the bomber command during the war."' That scuppered the Great Defender's case. The policeman involved went on to rise to high rank in the CID and took every opportunity to remind Joe of the case!

Regular appearances in the bear pit that can be a court of law breed a certain solidarity among the practitioners, especially those who specialise in pleading for the defence. Someone of the eminence of Joe Beltrami is quick to acknowledge the debt he owes to predecessors. Likewise the new star of the pleaders – Donald Findlay QC – was swift to express his friendship with and high opinion of Joe. Back in 1995 when the Sage of West Nile Street decided to cut down on court work and become a consultant with his firm, leaving the bulk of his work to his younger partners, Donald Findlay remarked: 'I always imagined that to get rid of Joe someone would have to take him outside and shoot him. A court won't be a court without Joe.' And indeed Joe Beltrami, who continued to be a major Glasgow legal figure, had the opportunity to repay that friendship when Donald Findlay's high-flying career hit some turbulence in 1999. Joe was a Roman Catholic and a man whose football fever took him mostly to Celtic Park and Firhill, but he was quick to come to the aid of Donald Findlay in his time of trouble. The high-profile QC never hid his humble origins in Cowdenbeath or his love for Rangers. But when he was unknowingly filmed singing the Sash at a party to celebrate a Rangers victory in a Cup Final, a mighty row broke out in the Press and television.

A slightly fuzzy picture of this eminent man, microphone in hand, singing a sectarian song splashed all over the front page of a tabloid started a massive outcry, and the top brief's own defence of his actions disappeared – crushed under the stinging surf of controversy. A widely experienced and mentally strong man, he still took hard the revulsion that his indiscretion caused. For a time he was down. Later he continued to say that in his view he had not done anything terribly wrong. 'I've always been pro the fans and just a punter at heart – just a bluenose – and I joined in.' He called the whole business 'nonsense' and pointed out the huge number of friends and colleagues who called him 'the most non-sectarian person they know'. But he had to resign his beloved job as vice-chairman of Rangers and there were demands that he be expelled from the Faculty of Advocates. The case for the defence needed to be developed. Step in the Defender. Joe Beltrami put together a team of legal brains and was forthright in talking to the Press. 'He made a mistake but has learned from it over the past few months. This whole matter must now be brought to an end in the interests of fairness.'

Donald Findlay had initially reeled at the public dressing-down his action had caused. But anyone who strides a courtroom and moulds the opinions of a jury has to be resilient. And the Rangers-loving lawyer with a passion for mutton-chop whiskers, Sherlock Holmes-style pipes, teddy-bear ties and other flamboyant attire weathered the storm. He is a man who likes to be liked and 12 months later he could walk outside the High Court in company with a *Sunday Herald* reporter as passers-by called out affectionately to him and he returned the banter. At the height of the controversy he had to endure insults wherever he went. As part of a programme for rebuilding his life he became a private pilot – becoming literally a high-flying legal eagle. But it was his work that kept him going; he needed the adrenaline of the courtroom. Just a few days after the story of his actions at the party broke, he was in court defending a female client who was accused of murdering her husband. Judging by his performance during the trial, no outsider would have believed the QC was in the middle of a personal crisis.

Back in early 1999 there had been speculation that the sectarian songs incident would ruin Donald Findlay professionally. It didn't happen. Instead he was given work by an enormous number of solicitors who would not normally have used his services. And he received hundreds of letters of support from Celtic supporters and Catholic organisations: a good sign of changing times in a city with a history of sectarian division. But the big worry was the reaction of the Faculty of Advocates when he was called to account. In the event he was reprimanded and fined £3500.

Findlay sees the result of violent and impoverished lives each working day and it is clear that he takes his cases personally. He says he seldom sleeps the night before his final address to the jury and makes a point of going down to the cells when a client has been jailed. And with the sort of cases that Donald Findlay specialises in, that is usually for life if the defence fails. 'Each case is different. It's not just a murder – it's a client who has put his or her entire trust in you and you don't betray that. I have never not gone down to the cells to see a client who has been convicted because, whatever they have done, their life is irrevocably changed and you know what the future has in store for them. I think if you don't feel any compassion for them you are a strange individual. You're awake constantly through many trials. If it's a difficult case it is going through your mind the whole time. The day I stand up and address a jury and my stomach isn't churning then I will just turn on my heel and walk out of court and never come back.'

A complex man, Donald Findlay always makes a good interview. He was particularly interesting when talking about rationalising the business of defending the seemingly indefensible. He says that the only people he would not defend are the ones who tell him they are guilty but blatantly request him to get them off. 'Not many do that, but I suppose some do lie through their teeth to get a defence.' He would defend the war criminals of Bosnia if asked. 'I would have defended Hitler, although the crime there was of such magnitude it is almost impossible to consider.

'But at Nuremberg, those on trial were entitled to a defence. It is my chosen role in life to provide that.' And if he had got Hitler acquitted? 'Then that would have been because the prosecution had failed, and I would have had to try very hard not to let the verdict alarm me. There can be an intellectual appreciation of a case which is overwhelmingly against a client. That's applying your mind to the evidence. But if you have a gut feeling someone is guilty you swallow it. You bury it as deeply as you can. You just have to. It's not for you to decide. You can't allow yourself to be the judge. You are an advocate, you are pleading a case, and you must sound convinced about it without saying: "I believe this man is innocent." You tread a very fine line.'

Later in this book I chronicle a series of spectacular court successes for Donald Findlay. Glasgow is indeed fortunate that it has had such a succession of great defenders in its always-busy courts – hard men of the law who continue to fight for justice and to keep the braying mob at bay.

12

DEATH BY FIRE
AND WAR ON THE STREETS

If there was one street in Glasgow that epitomised the problems of poverty and crime in a sink estate, it was Bankend Street, Ruchazie. There were 64 houses in the street, a familiar landmark for motorists driving into the city along the M8 from the east. This was a drab collection of crumbling homes, an uninviting place, an ugly blot on the landscape that created a hell to live in that was almost unimaginable to those who had not experienced it. At the end of the 1980s the city decided that it could not go on. Bankend Street and its neighbours were on a receiving end of a spectacular and costly makeover. Each house had £11,000 spent on it and the drabness of the buildings was replaced by neat balconies, attractive new roofs, and other bright external features. Well-intentioned politicians thought that at least some of the problems of the area would be ameliorated by waving a wand over the bricks and mortar. How wrong could they be? The story of the death of Bankend Street itself and the horrific deaths of its most famous residents underlines the immense problems of life in the East End of Glasgow in the '80s.

Four years on from the optimism of the makeover, bulldozers were sweeping away the homes that had so recently been improved. The occupancy rate had dropped to 50 per cent with one section of the street completely burned out. Anti-social tenants, combined with the systematic destructiveness of local youths and children, had created a new nightmare. Housing officials decided to cut their losses and get out. Local councillor Frank McAveety, one of the rising young stars of Labour local government, described the situation as a disaster brought about by a host of factors that were never addressed. According to him the council failed to consider the quality of tenants housed there, and the willingness of the local community to tackle some of the area's deep-seated social problems. He told *The Herald*: 'An anti-social element brought that improved stock to its knees, and we had to make a pretty dramatic decision, which had the support of the remaining tenants.'

The housing department had encountered a severe level of vandalism, on a scale seldom encountered on housing estates. The repair effort was almost completely tied up in coping with damage wrought by vandals rather than meeting the needs of the tenants. Security doors were battered down and whole heating systems stolen from empty houses. Councillor McAveety added: 'It's a genuine mistake that we didn't cope with these issues. We aren't just talking about young people in their 20s being involved. We are talking about youngsters between 13 and 14 years of age engaging in systematic destruction.'

He went on to say that intimidation had played a major part in the council's failure to deal with anti-social elements. Few people wanted to give evidence in court against neighbours who could give them serious problems. He argued: 'Peer pressure has to work. We have to marginalise the anti-socials.' The Depute Director of Housing at the time, Ronald MacDonald, who had been brought up in Ruchazie, said Bankend Street had always had a 'macho' reputation. There was no doubt that victimisation had been going on.

So the bulldozers moved in and a street that had been the site of mass murder crumbled to dust and into history. This street and its problems were background to one of the most evil – and controversial – acts in the criminal history of Glasgow. This was the site of the Ice-Cream Wars Murders in the early hours of

16 April 1984. The residents of Bankend Street who died were: James Doyle Snr, 53; James Doyle Jnr, 23; Tony Doyle, 14; Andrew Doyle, 18; their sister Christine Halleron, 25; and baby Mark Halleron, aged one. They were killed by a malicious, deliberately set fire in a crime that 17 years later is still making headlines.

The full story took some time to emerge. The first reports told that Christine Halleron and her young brother Anthony Doyle had died in the blaze and that doctors lost the fight to save little Mark Halleron. The fire had been started in a storage cupboard in the three-bedroom flat in Bankend Street. The cupboard had been used for keeping tyres and timber and once the flames had 'exploded' out of it they quickly flashed through the L-shaped corridor of the flat into the sleeping family's bedrooms. Nine people were trapped behind a wall of flame that night. Hardened detectives were said to be sickened by the callousness of the act. This was highlighted by the fact that on the night of the fire, the Doyles' flat was brimming over with family members celebrating the birth of a granddaughter days before. Young James, who died in the fire, had visited his wife Anne and new baby daughter Claire in Rutherglen maternity hospital before returning to 29 Bankend Street to spend the night.

The police were as outraged as the thousands of shocked Glaswegians. Detective Superintendent Norman Walker called the fire a 'bloody murderous' act. The trapped victims had little chance of escape and Mr Walker said it was the worst murder he had come across. To underline that this was no ordinary fire Charles Craig, joint head of the CID, had announced immediately that it was a murder inquiry. After killing Christine, Anthony and baby Mark, the intensity of the fire had left James Doyle Snr on a life-support machine in hospital and young James Doyle critical in the burns unit of the Royal Infirmary. His brothers Daniel, 28, and Andrew, 18, were also in the burns unit, seriously injured; and another brother, Stephen, 21, who fled the flames by jumping 40 feet from a window in the flat, had an operation in the Royal to repair a shattered leg. He also had serious back injuries. A senior policeman said: 'He is lucky to be alive'. Mrs Lillian Doyle, 52, received treatment for smoke inhalation and shock and was able to leave hospital for her daughter Linda's home in Meadowpark Street, Dennistoun. Neighbours had persuaded her to jump from a window-ledge.

Detective Walker was one of 40 officers involved in the murder investigation. He said: 'The fire could have been lit anytime between midnight and one o'clock. Whoever did this knew it could not be discovered.' 'Detectives,' said the *Herald*, 'are waiting to interview members of "the hard-working, decent family" to try to find a motive for the murders.' A murder headquarters was set up at Easterhouse Police Station and there was an appeal to anyone who had information or saw anything suspicious between midnight and 2 a.m. on Monday, 16 April. The reports said that the Doyles had lived in the flat for 20 years and were liked and respected by their neighbours. Mrs Elizabeth McKenzie, a 28-year-old mother of three who lived in a flat below the Doyles, said: 'I don't know who could have done such an evil and terrible thing. They have got hearts of gold and I just can't think of anyone who would harm them. They had no enemies as far as I know. I am so shocked I just can't believe that this has happened.' Mrs McKenzie's husband Albert had tried to get into the flat after they had been wakened by banging on the door. He told reporters: 'I tried to get into the flat, but smoke and flames were shooting out the door. There was no way anyone could have got in. I ran to the back of the flat and found Stephen shouting for help. He was lying in a pool of blood after cutting his arm jumping out of the window.' In a dramatic rescue attempt firemen wearing breathing apparatus stretchered survivors to safety.

One day later the death toll had risen to four. Twenty-five hours after the fire, young James Doyle died in the Royal from his injuries. His father and brothers Daniel and Andrew were still on life-support machines and critically ill in the Infirmary's intensive care unit. They were all too ill to be told of the deaths in the horror of Bankend Street. But some sinister overtones were beginning to emerge as detectives stepped up the hunt.

The men in charge of the investigation, Charles Craig and Norman Walker, were running into a brick wall in their search for East Enders ready to come forward with information – information that would establish the motive for this horrific crime. Three of the injured family were still too ill to talk to the police, though they had a bedside interview with 21-year-old Stephen whose life was not now in danger. The toll continued to rise, and four days later Andrew – who had briefly rallied, giving his mother hope that he might survive – had a relapse and died.

A motive was gently edging into the police frame. Andrew made his living as an ice-cream salesman touring the Garthamlock area in a van after taking out a franchise from the Marchetti Brothers of Maryhill. Despite police appeals and promises of confidentiality, the citizenry of the area had little to tell the detectives – but a picture of a feud was emerging. It turned out that prior to the fire Andrew had been attacked at least twice in his ice-cream van. In one attack he was fired on with a shotgun and in another he was savagely beaten up just outside his home after leaving the ice-cream van parked. And the toll was rising to six. James Snr had died in hospital. Smoke inhalation as much as burns from the flames had caused some of the Doyle deaths. A specialist from the Royal's burns unit explained that people who suffer a single injury of even 20-degree burns can live. But victims who are affected by a combination of burns and massive smoke inhalation are likely to die.

The next move in the police search for the killers was to get the *Evening Times* to join in the hunt and create a dramatic poster appealing to the public for assistance in solving the mystery of the mass murder. The posters were distributed to every possible outlet in the East End. Chief Supt Craig said: 'This is just what we need. If they can get anyone to come forward with information they will have been invaluable.' And 24 hours later his colleague Detective Supt Norman Walker was saying that the response was tremendous and that he was now confident the murderer would be caught. 'A few interesting lines of enquiry are being thrown up.' But Glasgow being Glasgow, there was a downside to all the public interest in this horrific murder – Ruchazie police were asked to investigate bogus collectors said to be cashing in on the wave of sympathy and trousering cash collected round the doors for the stricken family.

Eleven days after the fire the six victims were laid to rest at Old Monklands cemetery in Coatbridge – and senior detectives mingled with mourners in the search for a clue that could lead them to the culprit or culprits. Hundreds attended the funeral ceremony in St Phillips Church, Ruchazie and hundreds more waited silently outside. The local MP at the time, Hugh Brown, attended along with representatives from the regional and district councils. Also among the mourners was legendary Celtic and Scotland soccer star Danny McGrain, a friend of the family.

With the immediate shock of the crime receding, the nature of the ice-cream wars became the subject of more and more Press speculation. One *Evening Times* feature spelled out how sales could average up to £2000 a week – major money in the '80s – and how pirate operators could 'muscle in' on lucrative rounds using violence and intimidation. One legitimate trader, afraid to be identified, spelled out the scale of the problem. He was attacked by an axeman at his garage. His was a lucrative beat and heavies were noising him up, advising him to pack in the business and stay healthy. Lorenzo Boni of Bathgate, who operated a fleet of ice-cream vans, was a representative on the Ice-cream Alliance whose members had vans in most parts of Britain. He was up-front with the Press, telling reporters that he would not be surprised if a vendetta was the motive for the killings. He said that among other harassments, he and his drivers had suffered bricks through their windscreens, beatings, nails in tyres, road-blocks, and sugar in their petrol tanks. He sold up.

Back in the East End, the police case had built up to the point that two men were accused of murdering the Doyles by setting fire to their home. Thomas Campbell, 31, and Thomas Lafferty, 18, were remanded in custody at Glasgow Sheriff Court. The murder charges followed on to Campbell of Barlanark and Lafferty of Garthamlock appearing in the same court accused of attempting to murder Andrew Doyle and a 15-year-old Anne Wilson by firing a shot at them through the windscreen of their ice-cream van. They also faced charges of plotting to build up an ice-cream business by means of threats and intimidation. A few days later three other men were also charged. They were Joseph Steele, 22, and Gary Moore, 21, from Garthamlock and 31-year-old Thomas Gray from Carntyne. The charge against the three men was that while acting with two others they wilfully set fire to a cupboard door and the entrance to the house. The fire took effect, and the family residing there died as a result; and they murdered them. The murder charge against Lafferty was later abandoned, and in September 1984 Thomas Campbell, Thomas Gray, Gary Moore and Joseph Steele went on trial in the High Court accused of killing the six Doyles. This was 17 years ago – and from day one Thomas Campbell proclaimed his innocence. It was the start of a consistent campaign that would lead to years of on-and-off hunger strikes, roof-top protests, escapes and a constant war with the authorities with regard to the conditions under which he was held in various prisons in Scotland.

As evening papers do, the *Evening Times* had the first bite at the cherry reporting a trial that gripped Glasgow in much the way the Manuel trial had done years before. Even some of the international interest sparked by the mass murderer from Lanarkshire was repeated. The ice-cream wars had attracted the attention of the cinema and the whole background of what was going on in the schemes in the East End of Glasgow was big news on television and radio throughout Britain. The main charges alleged that

Thomas Campbell (31) of Barlanark Road, Barlanark; Thomas Gray (31) of Myreside Street, Carntyne; Joseph Steele (22) of Craiglockhart Street, Garthamlock; and Gary Moore (21) of Craigievar Street, Garthamlock wilfully set fire to a cupboard door and the entrance door of the house with a criminal disregard for the safety of the occupants. They denied the charges and lodged special defences of alibi and incrimination naming other persons.

Almost immediately on the start of the trial at the High Court in Glasgow it was said that Thomas Campbell claimed the police knew he was not responsible for the death blaze. He told the court he was only charged with murder to force him to say who had started the fire. According to him he was at home in bed with his wife on the night of the fire. His claims against the police had originally been made in a judicial examination held before a sheriff some months before. His defence council, Mr Donald Macaulay QC, asked the clerk of the court to read the judicial examination to the High Court jury. Before the Sheriff, Campbell had denied saying to the police that 'the fire at fat boy's was only meant to be a frightener that went too far'. The High Court heard that he had been asked if he had anything to say on the allegation that along with Thomas Lafferty, he had been in Bankend Street on the night of the fire. He replied, 'We weren't there. No way was I there, anyway.' At the judicial examination Campbell had been asked if he wished to incriminate anyone in the fire. He replied to the effect that if he knew who was responsible he would say, but that he didn't. He went on to claim that the police would drop the charges against him if he named the killer. And he yet again emphatically denied murdering the Doyles.

The trial was to go on for 27 days. It ended with the conviction of 'TC' Campbell and Steele for the murder of the Doyles. Earlier, Lord Kincraig had instructed the jury to return a not-guilty verdict on the murder charge against Gray, and the Crown had dropped the case against Moore and cleared him because of insufficient evidence. The jury of five men and ten women returned a total of

13 guilty verdicts against the accused in the case on a variety of other charges. The jury took eight hours to reach a verdict. Steele and 'TC' Campbell were described as 'vicious and dangerous' and given life sentences. For Campbell, the judge had ruled that life meant a minimum of 20 years in prison; no recommendation was made in the case of Steele. In addition to his murder conviction Campbell was jailed for 10 years after being found guilty of assault with intent to endanger the lives of Andrew Doyle and Anne Wilson during an armed attack on their ice-cream van. In his summing-up Lord Kincraig had warned the jury to put aside feelings of disgust and horror and concentrate only on the evidence. He said: 'Persons involved directly or indirectly in blasting off a shotgun at an ice-cream van in a public place are villains of the first degree. And those who set fire to the top flat in a tenement at a time when it is occupied and the occupants are liable to be asleep, and there is no means of escape except through the very place where the fire is started – causing the deaths of six persons, mostly young – are wicked and depraved persons, inhuman and evil.' Such people deserved no sympathy or consideration. He talked of 'dastardly deeds' and added: 'Put aside the feelings of disgust and horror which the evidence must have put in your minds and concentrate judicially and impartially on the evidence which connects any of the accused with these crimes.'

No matter the history of appeals, the fact is that the jury who sat through this long-running trial for weeks listened to the judge and found the police case against Campbell and Steele proved. But with hindsight, no one can deny that the evidence was largely circumstantial – with the major exception of the testimony of William Love, who claimed to have heard the accused planning the attack. This was evidence that he was later to claim had been forced out of him by the police and that he was lying. It was to form the basis of later appeals, of which there were many. And from day one of their conviction, Steele and Thomas 'TC' Campbell were steadfast in their claims of innocence. Neither hid the fact that they were hard men but this, according to them, was a crime they did not commit. Nonetheless, there was to be a whole series of failed appeals over the next 17 years.

The trial had been an expensive exercise: a few days after the verdicts were reached, the then Chief Constable of Strathclyde, Sir Patrick Hamill, said the police costs had reached £300,000. Forty officers were involved in the investigation and £62,000 had been paid out in overtime for detectives and other police personnel. This made it one of the most expensive murder investigations in the city's history. It was, incidentally, just one of the heavy costs the force had to bear in the mid-1980s. The miners' strike and a pay-rise meant that the force was strapped for cash and Sir Patrick warned the region's police committee that lack of cash would have an adverse effect on patrolling in the housing schemes. Ironic, in view of the nature of the ice-cream wars!

With the shackles of a live trial removed, the papers began to spell out to anyone who didn't know it the villainous background of 'TC' and Steele. Campbell, described as nearly six feet tall, slender and with a receding hairline, openly boasted about having a split personality. He could sit chatting in a local pub being charming and pleasant to his companions and then go to the toilet and take out a weapon and strike at someone whose face didn't fit. Not too surprisingly, this tendency to mindless violence made many shun his company, preferring to move out rather than get involved in the lottery of his mood-swings.

Violence had always played a role in Campbell's life – even as a youngster growing up in Rigby Street in Carntyne. He was a member of the Gaucho, a local gang, and in fights with rivals like the Powrie he would lead from the front – staying in scraps till the bitter end. Petty crime and hold-ups became a way of life, and at one stage responsibility for any robbery in the area was placed by rumour at his door. His reputation was built from an early age. And from the start of his criminal life, he ran with the Steele brothers, James, John and Joseph, who grew up with him as near-neighbours. All four were to become no strangers to the inside of Scotland's prisons. Gang exploits put Campbell behind bars in 1972: he had led the Gaucho on a night of terror when they invaded a street in Haghill armed with knives, meat cleavers and bottles. Windows were smashed and a family assaulted. Two men locked themselves in a house through fear of Campbell and the gang charged through the street shouting 'Gaucho rule' and 'Kill'.

And in 1980 Campbell had stood trial charged with helping three of Glasgow's toughest criminals escape from Barlinnie in a commando-style operation organised from outside. He was also accused of providing the escapees with food and safe houses, but was acquitted. Freed with him on that occasion was Thomas Lafferty – known as 'the Shadow' because he was seldom far from Campbell's side – a man whose name crops up consistently in the long-running tale. Campbell's brother-in-law, he was a self-confessed alcoholic who deliberately played up his unreliable nature in court to suggest that no-one would ever have trusted him on a violent escapade.

Out of jail after the Gaucho episode, Campbell was soon back trying to create a one-man crime wave, without making much in the way of money to show for it – until he moved in on the ice-cream van game. He couldn't drive but instead sat at home directing operations and raking in the cash. There was no doubt that professional criminals were muscling in on the vans as a business front for laundering dirty money, as well as selling drugs, stolen liquor and other easily resaleable stolen goods like cigarettes and confectionery. But the legitimate traders had to be frightened off, and after the Doyle trial there was speculation that Campbell was the professional hard man used by other shadowy figures to drive away the honest operators – a theme that was to emerge again later in the saga. In the short term, though, Campbell had a problem. The cash generated by the vans was significant and he had plans to expand to other schemes like Castlemilk in the southside. He acquired the notion that the Civic Government (Scotland) Act which had been used to change the system of licensing taxis would soon take action on the licensing of ice-cream vans. If this happened he needed to get more vans under his control in a hurry or he could be left out in the cold. This was one of the driving factors of the ice-cream wars. But it was based on a misconception – at the time of the death blaze the authorities had no plans for large-scale intervention in the ice-cream van trade.

In jail, Campbell – still protesting his innocence – was a difficult man. In June 1986 he was cleared of punching a chief officer at Peterhead top security prison. He was alleged to have lashed out with his fist when he heard that a visit from his family had been cancelled because of investigations into a riot the previous night. The sheriff said he entertained a doubt about the prosecution case and found Campbell not guilty of assault. But at the same time he threw out Campbell's claim that he had been beaten up and kicked by a squad of eight officers in retribution for the riot, resulting in a stomach injury. Campbell's health gave concern of a different kind in 1987, when he again indulged in what seems to be a passion for hunger strikes – something that has marked his time in jail. This time it was to protest about being moved from Barlinnie to Peterhead. After he went on a liquids-only diet he was taken to the prison hospital and given 24-hour nursing care, though the authorities had no plans to force-feed him. He also planned action in the European Court of Human Rights in connection with alleged interference with his mail and other infringements, and won damages of £250 as compensation for the authorities allowing him to suffer an attack of bed-bugs in his cell.

Nor was his not-guilty verdict on the charge of assaulting the prison officer the end of that episode. A determined Campbell pursued his claim and in October 1989 he was awarded £4000 in damages against the then Secretary of State for Scotland, Malcolm Rifkind. Campbell had claimed £40,000 but after three days of evidence a civil jury made the lower award. They said they were satisfied that Campbell had sustained injuries from the 'wrongful actions of prison officers'. It was admitted on behalf of the Secretary of State that Campbell had suffered a ruptured bowel for which he needed an operation in Aberdeen Royal Infirmary, and that the injury had happened when a number of officers were in his cell. It was claimed that Campbell had suddenly attacked the officer when he told him of the suspended visits. A violent struggle took place in which Campbell and other officers fell together in a heap on the floor. Campbell claimed he was beaten with riot sticks and stamped on. The prison officer, by then retired, said that the attack on him was 'out of character' and that Campbell later apologised. He also said that Campbell was not involved in the escape-bid that had sparked the trouble. A prisoner gave evidence that he had watched through his cell's 'Judas Hole' as warders with sticks beat up Campbell.

In the same year the case took a startling new turn when Campbell's lawyer said he believed he had unearthed fresh evidence in his fight against the minimum 20-year sentence. John Carroll included his findings in a petition lodged with the Secretary of State seeking an appeal at Edinburgh's High Court of Justiciary. The moves were announced as Campbell entered the ninth day of an alleged attempt to starve himself to death. But this was played down by the Scottish Office, who said: 'A prisoner at Shotts has been refusing food for 11 days. But he is buying food from the prison canteen. His condition is giving no concern to the medical staff.'

Mr Carroll said: 'I have discovered that a witness in the trial of Campbell had three previous convictions for attempting to pervert the course of justice. This is important evidence.' The witness was Billy Love, a Glasgow man who was then living in London with his wife and three children. Love was said to have given a tape-recorded statement to an English barrister and Mr Carroll claiming that CID officers in Glasgow induced him to make statements in return for arranging bail on charges of armed robbery. He also claimed that he was threatened by a depute procurator fiscal that unless he spoke in court about the statements he had made to the police he would end up on the same charges as Campbell. But he later changed his story again, saying that what he had said in court was true.

The appeal plea was rejected by the Secretary of State, who ruled that no further appeal could be considered just because a key witness changes his story. Mr Carroll had already taken the case to Europe. He told the European Commission on Human Rights that Campbell had been denied the right to a fair hearing at his appeal by being handcuffed throughout, but this was dismissed on technicalities at the Commission stage and failed to reach the Court of Human Rights. A petition to the Scottish Secretary claiming failure of the appeal court to properly apply its mind to one of the appeal grounds was also rejected.

Campbell, once the self-styled Emperor of Carntyne and perhaps more flamboyant than Steele, tended to get more space in the papers – but they were equally determined to declaim their innocence, no matter how long it took. In 1993 it was Steele's turn to make the headlines. He slipped his police escort on a visit to his sick mother in her home in Garthamlock and was whisked off to London by friends. It was hardly a high-tech escape – he had pretended to go to the toilet and then did a runner. In London he told the Press: 'I am not the beast that was portrayed in the media' and revealed that he had refused parole to prove his innocence. He said: 'If I admit my guilt to the parole board I know I could be a free man a lot sooner but I would rather serve 15 to 20 years to finally prove my innocence than walk out a guilty man.' This escapade ended when he gave himself up to the authorities after staging a dramatic protest outside the walls of Barlinnie. He was dropped off around 4 p.m. by friends and then climbed halfway up a 60-foot surveillance and lighting tower only yards from the main gate and began shouting his innocence. An earlier escape from Saughton had ended after he had glued himself to the railings of Buckingham Palace to highlight his case.

By now Campbell and Steele were becoming a national story and were known as the 'Glasgow Two'. A spectacular series of miscarriages of justice in England was helping to fuel their case. Indeed, Paddy Hill, one of the freed Birmingham Six, made a hush-hush visit to Campbell in the Barlinnie Special Unit. Back in London, Hill said: 'It was good to meet with Tommy Campbell and discuss the case with him first hand. There are certainly parallels between his case and mine.' He went on to comment: 'But the system up there seems to be a lot more rotten than the one here in England.' The meeting between Hill and Campbell took place shortly before the Special Unit closed down and 'TC' was transferred to Shotts. Hill was just one of a number of wrongly accused south of the border to give support to the Glasgow Two.

Late in 1994 the saga took yet another twist, when it was revealed in the *Evening Times* that evidence that could have been vital to appeals by the Two had been destroyed by the police or the fiscal service. Each blamed the other for the destruction of material relating to William Love's retraction of his original evidence. Defence lawyer John Carroll had asked the procurator fiscal for the original police notebooks, case notes, operational sheets, witness lists, laboratory papers and other court productions, but was told that they had been destroyed. This was to be just a set-back in John Carroll's remarkable fight for justice for Steele and Campbell. At the time Thomas Campbell was making legal history by being the last prisoner to be transferred out of the Special Unit as it was closed down. The Unit had housed some of Scotland's most violent criminals without a serious outbreak of trouble, but a report from a working party concluded that it was no longer performing its function, spelling out the end of an experiment that had been watched by penal reformers worldwide. Campbell went to his new prison with the comment: 'The Special Unit gave me a lifeline. Now it is closed, I feel that my hopes of release and some kind of life in prison are over.'

The next year it looked as if fate was moving towards freedom for the Glasgow Two. But it was the start of what was to be the most bitter-sweet period in the whole astonishing case. The then Scottish Secretary Michael Forsyth decided to refer the 12-year-old convictions to the Appeal Court. This effectively overruled the previous Crown Office decision that there was 'insufficient reliable evidence' to justify proceedings against the key witness at the 1984 trial, William Love, who has repeatedly admitted that he gave perjured evidence. This led to a spell of freedom for the Two. First, at the High Court in Edinburgh, Joe Steele was granted interim liberation until his appeal against the conviction was heard. He wept. The next week Thomas Campbell was also celebrating freedom – however transitory. He was granted bail pending the outcome of the appeal. According to *The Herald* this was the first signal that the legal establishment's 'previously impregnable citadel of certainty over the convictions may be built on sand'. The later course of the appeal was to show that this was a tad optimistic.

But the same report did highlight the bitterness with which the establishment had fought its rearguard action to preserve the convictions at all costs. It went on to point out that Campbell and Steele had never been supported by the formidable team assembled for the 'Free Paddy Meehan' campaign. It had been down to John Carroll, some high-profile journalists and family and friends to fight the alleged injustice.

When the appeal did start, Graham Bell QC told the court that William Love had been an essential witness for the Crown but that: 'he has since made statements indicating his evidence at the trial was untrue'. We had again arrived at the nub of the matter – the claim that the alleged overheard pub conversation had never taken place. Three months later there was fury in court when Campbell and Steele listened as their appeal was thrown out. According to reports, they were visibly shaken as the three senior judges voted 2–1 that the appeal be refused. They were then led away from the Court of Criminal Appeal in Edinburgh, flanked by prison officers. In the packed public gallery behind them crowds were ordered to be silent as family and friends of the convicted killers roared disapproval. Policemen rushed into the court to calm the disorder. Steele had married during his freedom and his wife was pregnant. TC was about to become a father again. Steele's mother Margaret wept on hearing the news.

Each judge had placed his decision in a sealed envelope which was opened by Lord Cullen in court. Lord Cullen said he was minded to turn down the appeal as the Crown had produced compelling arguments to refute the appeals claim. Lord McCluskey disagreed, and it was Lord Sutherland who gave the final decision that sent them back to jail after more than a year of freedom. Apart from the dispute over Love's own evidence, his sister Agnes Carlton, who was cited as a witness in 1984, also signed an affidavit that she was giving evidence not heard earlier. She told the appeal hearing that on the night an ice-cream van was blasted by a shotgun she had seen her brother, Love, firing the shots. But Lord Cullen said that he was not satisfied that her evidence could be submitted for the appeal.

In a leader the next day the *Evening Times* made some pertinent points. It pointed out that similar cases in England had resulted in quashed convictions or retrials. A change in the law had allowed an appeal on the grounds of a witness changing evidence. William Love, whose evidence was crucial to the 1984 conviction, did precisely that. Yet the new procedure requires corroboration from a second source and a 'test of reasonable explanation'. And here the appeal foundered. 'Lords Cullen and Sutherland sided against Lord McCluskey and decided that the appeal should be refused. Without hearing fresh evidence. . . . Both Campbell and Steele have steadfastly denied their guilt to the extent of refusing parole, staging hunger strikes and spectacular escapes. That in itself is no guarantee of innocence, but it has been consistent. The court's refusal to hear any new evidence might make legal sense. But it leaves a huge question-mark over Scottish justice.' A verdict that many observers would agree with.

Back behind bars 'TC' pulled a new stroke. He claimed he knew the identity of the real killer. Because of legal reasons this man could not be named. Campbell said: 'I know who he is and I have met him. I have got evidence that the authorities knew at the time who did it.' He claimed the man was a shadowy figure known to the police who had been implicated in other murders. A new complexity in a complex case. And if TC still couldn't keep quiet in jail, neither could his supporters: the failure of the appeal spurred them on. Glasgow MP Jimmy Wray wanted a Commons debate to discuss his call for a retrial. Mr Wray had campaigned for the Two even before their release on bail in 1996. He had written to three successive Scottish Secretaries – Malcolm Rifkind, Ian Lang and Michael Forsyth – calling for their cases to be reviewed. It didn't happen.

But the pair were granted interim liberation in late 2001 by appeal court judges after a referral by the Criminal Cases Review Commission.

Complete freedom and justice was merely postponed for the Glasgow Two. The wrangling over their appeal went through some convoluted and lengthy legal processes, but finally, in March 2004, TC Campbell and Joseph Steele had their convictions quashed by Scotland's second most senior judge, the Lord Justice Clerk, Lord Gill, sitting with Lord Maclean and Lord Macfayden. It was their third appearance before appeal judges. New evidence had been produced that threw doubt on statements made by detectives in the original trial and the two men who had spent 16 years behind bars for murder, all the time protesting their innocence, were belatedly vindicated. But this bizarre affair was not yet completely over. The decision of the Appeal Court implied a police frame-up, something that could lead to an investigaton. And the final question remains unanswered – who killed the Doyles?

13

PADDY MEEHAN,
MURDER AND BOOKS GALORE

The tangled underworld of Glasgow is peopled with a rich mixture of seedy characters who interact in a remarkable way. A pebble thrown into the murky waters creates waves washing over a selection of names whose paths cross as they pursue their criminal enterprises. The Paddy Meehan saga is the ultimate proof of that. Meehan went to jail in 1969 wrongfully convicted of the murder of an Ayr pensioner. He died in a Swansea hospital in August 1994. What happened in between became a story as notorious as any in Scottish legal history – a story thick with the names of some of the city's most infamous villains. Before it was over there were accusations of police planting evidence, of an establishment cover-up and even the involvement of the secret services.

The tale began in 1969 when the West of Scotland was horrified by the murder of Mrs Rachael Ross, a 72-year-old pensioner, in the house in Ayr she shared with her ex-bookmaker husband Abraham. Intruders had broken into their home and tied up the wealthy couple, bludgeoning Mrs Ross who sustained horrific head injuries and later died in hospital. Her husband was left beside her, and the couple were not found for a further 24 hours. The high profile of the murder and the fact that pensioners were involved put a lot of pressure on the police to find the culprits. Not for the first time, the reaction was to question criminals with 'form'. Paddy Meehan was a well-known safebreaker suspected of being in the area on the night of the murder. Police questioned him, setting in train events that were to end in a dramatic shoot-out in Glasgow. Meehan told the police that he had been in Stranraer on the night in question in the company of Jim Griffiths. Griffiths was also well known to the Scottish police: he had a record of violence and a pathological fear of imprisonment – a dangerous mixture. When the police approached him to question him about the events in Ayr he went berserk. He met them with a hail of bullets and embarked on a daylight rampage through the streets of Glasgow. He had a rifle and a shotgun, and fired indiscriminately into a children's playground. He shot nine men – one fatally – two women, a child and a police officer. Finally he was shot down by the police in a house in Springburn after a dramatic street-chase worthy of Hollywood or Chicago.

Strathclyde, Britain's second biggest force, has a first-class record when it comes to the use of firearms. And there was no doubt that they had to be drawn in a case like this. The chase had started at Griffiths' lodgings in a house off Great Western Road. The wounded policeman had been caught in the gunfire as he arrived at the house. A siege began but Jim Griffiths escaped out the back of the building, commandeered a car at gunpoint, went to a bar and demanded a bottle of brandy, and then shot a news vendor who later died. He then commandeered a lorry and turned up in Springburn, where he broke into a flat and had started firing shots out of the window when the police caught up with him. He had to be stopped before more blood was shed. Armed with revolvers, two officers, Malcolm Finlayson and Ian Smith, crept up the stairs to the flat where the madman was holed up. At the time, there was a clampdown on the identity of the brave policemen, but the details later emerged. Griffiths was desperate, trapped and with nothing to lose. It was an extreme situation. The police prised open the letterbox in the front door of the flat and – perhaps noticing what was going on – the killer turned to face the door. Chief Inspector Malcolm Finlayson decided to try to maim him and fired a shot through the letterbox. He aimed at Griffiths' shoulder but the bullet ricocheted into his heart. The madness was over. Malcolm Finlayson was later awarded the MBE and Ian Smith the BEM. It was the first time in Scotland that an armed policeman had shot and killed in such an incident.

Detective Chief Superintendent Tom Goodall, then head of the CID and the man who had played a leading role in the apprehension of many of the city's worst villains, told a news conference: 'The full facts surrounding his death will be reported as soon as possible to the Procurator Fiscal.' Mr Goodall praised the actions of his men throughout the incident. He said the police were armed to prevent members of the public being shot. 'If they had to use their guns to do that, then that is alright.' He went on to say that all the officers involved had acted in a most commendable manner and that 'I think we can be proud of the force'. A full statement was later made by the Crown Office – a statement that was perhaps unwise and would lead to accusations after the trial. Part of the lengthy statement said: 'The Crown Office can confirm that with the death of Griffiths and the apprehension of Patrick Connolly Meehan, the police are no longer looking for any other person suspected of implication in the incident concerning Mr and Mrs Ross at Ayr.' From this distance in time it looks as if a little pre-trial triumphalism was taking place. Incidentally, in early reports of the case, and indeed in official documents, Paddy's name was often spelled as Meechan. But latterly the style Meehan prevailed.

On the first of August 1969, 34-year-old Griffiths was buried in an unmarked pauper's grave in the Linn Cemetery in Cathcart in Glasgow's southside. His family in Rochdale had disowned him when he was 17 after he broke into his brother's house. His body had lain in the Glasgow police mortuary and his funeral became the responsibility of the city corporation after his father had declined to travel from his home in Northamptonshire. When the hearse arrived at the cemetery only the gravediggers were waiting.

There were no flowers or wreaths. The undertaker said a short prayer. On the same day on the other side of the city, William Hughes – the 65-year-old news vendor shot by Griffiths during his rampage through the streets of Glasgow – was laid to rest in Sandymount cemetery, Springboig.

The actions of Griffiths had helped point the finger at Meehan himself. If the dubious duo hadn't been involved in this particular housebreaking, why had Griffiths panicked and taken such an extreme reaction? Seemingly overlooked was the fact that the Englishman had been on the run for months before the Ross murder. And it is interesting to note that in those days of inch-high headlines and page after page of detail on the important crimes, the start of what was to become one of the most celebrated cases in Scottish criminal history was marked only by a few paragraphs tucked away down the page.

Before the actual legal proceedings had begun, Abraham Ross had decided to face the Press cameras from his hospital bed so that the public – already responding well to police appeals for help – could see the extent of his injuries and realise how badly he and his wife had been treated. He sat up in bed in a screened-off ward in Ayr County Hospital. His face showed dramatically the marks of violence which had been meted out to him by his assailants, both masked, who according to senior detectives had acted with quite unnecessary force and brutality. The skin round the old man's wrists was burned where his bonds had cut into his flesh as he struggled to free himself during the 24 hours he and his wife lay undiscovered in their home in Blackburn Place, Ayr. The police had referred to 'sadism' in connection with the assaults. Rachael Ross had died 17 hours after she was found unconscious by Susan Grant, the couple's daily help, when she arrived for work on the Monday morning after that fateful weekend. Between 50 and 60 friends attended the funeral of Mrs Ross at the Western Necropolis, Maryhill. While they mourned, Detective Superintendent David Struthers, who was leading the hunt for the killers, was also in

Glasgow conferring with senior police officers. More than 100 detectives were helping with the inquiries.

At the end of September, at a High Court pleading diet in Ayr, three charges were preferred against Meehan, said to be aged 42 and of Rutherglen Road, Glasgow. Joe Beltrami represented him and on his behalf tendered pleas of not guilty to all three charges, which were:

That on 6 July 1969, while acting with another person, Meehan:

1. Broke into the house at 2 Blackburn Place, Ayr and assaulted Abraham Ross, aged 67, punched him on the face and body, struck him on the shoulder and buttock with a sharp instrument, and bound him with rope and nylon stockings to his severe injury.
2. Assaulted Mrs Rachael Ross, aged 72, dragged her from her bed, put her on the floor, placed his knee on her chest, and bound her with rope and nylon stockings, as a result of which she died in Ayr County Hospital on July 8, and he murdered her.
3. Stole £2000 in money and a number of travellers' cheques.

Joe Beltrami, the Sage of West Nile Street, who was starting a relationship with the case that would continue of many years – ultimately seeing Meehan granted a Royal pardon and an intriguing feud between lawyer and client – intimated a special plea of impeachment and alibi.

The trial was not to take place in Ayr but at the High Court in Edinburgh and was slated to take around a week. But Meehan pulled a stroke even before it began. He presented a petition seeking that the 'truth drug' be administered. The *Herald* reported that the application to have the drug used on himself was believed to be without precedent in Britain, though it was already in fairly regular use in the United States as an aid to criminal investigations.

Had Meehan been at liberty, it was said, he would have had the freedom to administer the drug himself, but as he was in custody pending trial an application was necessary. The petition seeking the use of the drug, a composition of sodium pentathol and methydrene, was heard in open court by three judges. The application was an early indication that Meehan would continue with his pleas of total innocence. But the judges sitting in Edinburgh rejected the unusual request.

The Crown cited 110 witnesses and the trial was to go ahead on the date fixed. At one stage Joe Beltrami considered the possibility of asking for a postponement, saying that he had not had sufficient time to study the final indictment. However, the trial started, with advocates Nicholas Fairbairn and John Smith acting for the defence and Ewan Stewart QC leading for the prosecution. Joe Beltrami had chosen the flamboyant Fairbairn and the late John Smith to defend in the High Court. Nicky, of course, went on to a spectacular career in the law and as a Tory politician, while John Smith became a reforming leader of the Labour party and a man surely only denied the premiership by his untimely death in 1994 from heart trouble.

Early in the trial Nicky Fairbairn confirmed that Meehan was pleading not guilty to all of the charges except one dealing with a passport, and repeated the plea of incrimination – claiming that if a murder was committed it was not by Meehan but by Ian Waddell, an untried prisoner in Barlinnie Prison, and Samuel Philips whose whereabouts were said to be unknown. Abraham Ross appeared in court with a bandage over his right eye, a result of the attack. He said he was a director of the West End bingo club in Paisley and travelled regularly between Paisley and Ayr in that connection. He carried a fair amount of money, some of which he kept in Ayr. He told of falling asleep on the Saturday night. Mr Ross said: 'The next thing I remember was somebody coming at me and diving right on top of me. My wife was screaming and moaning. It was like a nightmare. I struggled with him and I could just see that my assailant was wearing a transparent black nylon hood over his head and black nylon tights.'

Mr Ross said that for this reason he was unable to recognise his assailant, but though a blanket had been placed over his head he was aware that there were two men. When the man with whom he was struggling called to the other, 'Pat, get this ---- off me', he received a further knock on the head and was unable to continue resistance. In reply to the prosecution he said that his assailant was called Jim by the other man. Before the men left they bound his wife and himself by the hands and feet with rope and nylon stocking and left them lying on the floor. He said his wife succeeded in reaching the phone but that it was out of order. 'We were unable to free ourselves,' he added, 'and shouted for help all day long on the Sunday, but though we heard people passing no one heard us and we were in a pretty bad state. Eventually the daily help came on the Monday morning and we were taken to hospital. I did not see my wife again.'

During the cross-examination Mr Fairbairn was given permission to call Ian Waddell into court. He handed Waddell a piece of paper and asked him to repeat various phrases including 'shut up, shut up, we'll send an ambulance'. This was an attempt to discredit the previous identification of Meehan's voice by the witness. Mr Ross agreed that the voice was similar to that heard in the identification parade he had attended, but because of the interval of time he could not be certain.

The story of the identification parade was told dramatically in court. Detective Superintendent David Struthers said that when a warrant was presented at his house Meehan said, 'You are making the biggest mistake of your life', later adding: 'What have I to go in an identification parade for? They are only the two girls I picked up.' (This was a reference to girls to whom Griffiths and Meehan had given a lift near Kilmarnock on the night of the murder, when they claimed they were returning from Stranraer.) When he was cautioned and charged the same day he replied: 'You are making a horrible mistake. I know absolutely nothing about it.' A detective sergeant told the court of the identification parade he had conducted at the Central Police Office in Glasgow. The parade consisted of six men, the accused being the first in the line. Abraham Ross, the assaulted man, asked the detective to get the men in the parade to repeat the words 'shut up, shut up, I'll get an ambulance, all right' – the words he said he had heard one of the assailants use in reply to his wife's pleadings. 'When the accused spoke these words,' the witness said, 'Ross staggered back, obviously shaken and said "That's him." He was on the verge of collapse and had to be more or less carried from the room.' Meehan's reply to this was, 'Oh sir, you've got the wrong man, honest.'

The identification parade was to be crucial in the eventual conviction of Meehan. But in the long years after the trial it was to be challenged by Meehan's supporters, who campaigned for his pardon claiming that Ross had been tipped a wink as to whom the police thought was the guilty man. Scraps of paper from the Ross house, found in Griffiths' car coat and mentioned at the trial, were also later alleged to have been planted by the police. However, back in 1969 in the High Court in Edinburgh after Mr Ross' evidence, the two girls who had been given a lift on the night of the crime spoke of the car coming from the direction of Ayr. At another identification parade one identified Meehan as the passenger and the other said the driver addressed him as Pat.

When Meehan first entered the witness box Mr Fairbairn asked him: 'Had you anything to do with the robbery and murder in Ayr on July 6?' Meehan replied: 'I was never at any time involved in that robbery and murder and I never set eyes on Mr Ross till I saw him in the identity parade.' Nicky Fairbairn went on to ask whether or not Meehan had set foot in Ayr that night and was told that he hadn't. But Paddy admitted that he might well have passed through Ayr on his way back from Stranraer during the early hours of 6 July, although he was trying to sleep while Griffiths drove. He told the court that the purpose of the trip to Stranraer was to 'look over' the motor-car registration office there with a view to breaking in at a later date and stealing a supply of registration books. These, he said, were to be used in the sale of cars stolen by Griffiths. He did not like the look of the office, though, and after visiting a restaurant, several public houses and the harbour they called at a hotel outside Stranraer with a view to stealing cameras. They had to wait till the lights went out but after Griffiths had broken into a van in the parking place they decided to return to Glasgow.

They left Stranraer about 2 a.m. and just outside Kilmarnock came across a young girl, obviously in distress, at the side of the road and offered her a lift. She said she had been put out of a white car by two young men who continued the journey with her girlfriend. Meehan said he and Griffiths invited the girl into the car and, travelling at speeds of more than 100 miles an hour, were able to overtake the white car and reunite the two girls whom they drove to their homes in Kilmarnock. When Meehan arrived home about 5 a.m. he told his wife what had happened. He went on to tell the court that he eventually learned from newspapers or television that a murder had been committed in Ayr around that time. He said his wife and daughter were upset at the brutal killing and his daughter said: 'Daddy, maybe the men in the white car had something to do with this. You should phone the police.'

'I didn't want to get involved but she insisted and I said I would phone the police without telling them my name.' He phoned saying he had a friend who might be able to identify the two young men. In reply to Mr Fairbairn, Meehan said the reason he did not then disclose his name was that he was in a delicate position because the police had been searching high and low for Griffiths for five or six months. Mr Fairbairn then made a telling point, asking: 'supposing for a moment you were the man who had committed the murder. Does that mean you made a call to the police disclosing the name of two girls who could probably identify you?' Meehan replied to the effect that like everyone else, he was disgusted at 'this filthy crime'. Later he again phoned the police and named the two girls. He left that night with Griffiths for England but soon returned. He added that although Griffiths was a man on the run, neither of them had intended to flee the country. Meehan was also questioned about the presence on his shoes of small stones similar to those covering the garage roof of the bungalow in Ayr. He said that at one time he had been employed in a store selling felting of the type found on the roof, and that accounted for the stones or gravel.

Examined by the prosecution, Meehan said that for some time he had been employed to install security devices in private houses and that he made around a tenner a day. He was asked what Griffiths did when the police came to interview him, and replied 'as far as I know he started shooting'. He denied knowing that Griffiths had a gun. The court then heard of telephone conversations between Tom Goodall and Griffiths in which the Englishman said he knew the identity of the guilty men. But he would not give himself up or name the men.

Next the Crown took on the allegation of incrimination. Ian Waddell was brought into court, and a lorry driver cited as a witness said he had been drinking with Waddell, spending the night of 5 July – until 10 a.m. on 6 July – in his company in Glasgow. Some allegations of a different hue came before the court when evidence of an alleged confession made to him in Barlinnie was given by Robert McCafferty, who was then an untried prisoner. He said that he was talking with other untried prisoners in the exercise yard and speculating on what sentences they might get if found guilty. One of them said, 'You think you're bad, just look at Paddy Meehan in for the Ayr murder.' McCafferty continued, 'When I turned round, Waddell, who had joined us, said: "how do you think I feel? It was me that done it." ' McCafferty asked if he was joking and Waddell said: 'No, what can I do if the police make a bloomer?' McCafferty went on to deplore the old couple having been left bound on the floor and alleged that Waddell replied, 'Phillips phoned but he only called the operator.' Waddell was brought into court and Lord Grant warned him that he did not need to answer any question he thought might incriminate him. Asked by Mr Fairbairn if he had ever used the words 'shut up, shut up, we'll get an ambulance' – a phrase alleged to have been used by one of the intruders – Waddell refused to answer.

But at the end of the five days of evidence the jury preferred the matters that pointed to Meehan's guilt – in particular the identification parade – rather than the defence submissions. They took almost two hours to reach a verdict by a majority. Even at the start of Meehan's troubled journey from conviction to Royal Pardon there were dissenting voices ready to argue his innocence after a trial filled with confusing claim and counter-claim. Lord Grant had directed the jury to find that incrimination had not been established. According to him there was not even remote evidence which would entitle them to do so. He also said they were not to be concerned with Griffiths' final hours or the manner of his death. 'You are trying the accused on the evidence you have heard in this court and on that evidence alone. Evidence of what a dead man said, not being subject to cross-examination, must be looked at with particular care,' he added. He pointed out that the evidence was largely circumstantial but they must look at the cumulative effect of the evidence as a whole. Meehan, said the judge, was a man who travelled about the countryside at nights on mysterious errands while earning £8 or £9 a day from the legitimate trade of going into people's houses and installing safety devices – a sort of Jekyll and Hyde existence. He was a self-confessed liar and crook. Be that as it may, Paddy Connolly Meehan's reaction to his sentence of imprisonment for life was clear. 'I am innocent of this crime and so is Griffiths. You have made a terrible mistake.'

Meehan left the court to start what was to be seven years of hell, much of it spent in solitary confinement protesting his innocence almost on a daily basis. The end of a curious trial started years of wrangling between lawyers, journalists and the legal establishment. Reading the trial reports more than 30 years on, it is easy to see why the defence felt that Lord Grant was on occasion tending to lean in the direction of the prosecution. The reports tell of the occasion when Meehan denied prosecution suggestions of his involvement by declaiming his innocence. Ewan Stewart then said to him: 'You are a self-confessed liar, aren't you?' Paddy replied to the effect that he had asked some months ago to be given the truth drug and be interrogated under its influence. Without using the courtesy title of Mr, Lord Grant intervened sarcastically: 'Can't you tell the truth without having a truth drug, Meehan?' And there were other occasions on which the defence felt they were witnessing partiality. However, that decision in Edinburgh became one of the most spectacular miscarriages of justice in Scottish criminal history. But it was a story never to have a totally satisfactory end.

In Peterhead prison Meehan was soon at odds with the authorities. In his view he was innocent, and if he shouldn't be in prison he would take no part in doing prison chores. The answer was to dump him in solitary, although he was still having visits from Joseph Beltrami and still protesting his innocence. In his book on the case, *A Deadly Innocence,* Beltrami noted that Meehan was turning against him. Not too unreasonable, thought the lawyer, since Meehan was innocent but in jail. Greatly to his credit this did nothing to stop the Glasgow lawyer fighting for years to help win Meehan his freedom. The move to secure justice for Paddy really got into top gear when in 1972 he wrote to the broadcaster and writer Ludovic Kennedy, who was known to have an interest in miscarriages of justice. And contacts that Joe Beltrami had made with underworld figures who knew the score – including Arthur Thompson – convinced the lawyer that Meehan was innocent. Few who study the whole saga can fail to be impressed with the energy and effort put into the case by Joe Beltrami. Meehan also wrote to famous Glasgow lawyers Ross Harper and Len Murray: Beltrami was magnanimous about this move, acknowledging that several legal heads were better than one on a complex issue like this.

Kennedy and Beltrami met and got on well and Kennedy set about launching a Free Paddy Meehan committee. Beltrami joined, along with David Scott of Scottish Television (later to join the *Herald* group's ill-fated *Sunday Standard*, which was published from 1981 to 1983), lawyers Ross Harper, Len Murray, David Burnside and Bert Kerrigan, and a reporter from the *Sunday Times* who was a friend of Kennedy. Ludovic Kennedy also wrote a book on the Meehan saga entitled *A Presumption of Innocence*. And his investigations into the case led him to lay the blame for the crime at the door of William 'Tank' McGuinness – a notorious Glasgow underworld figure and a noted 'tie-up' merchant, according to Paddy Meehan. In Kennedy's version, McGuinness was accompanied by Ian Waddell when they broke into the Ross bungalow.

But there was to be yet another twist in this most convoluted of tales when, after Meehan was pardoned in 1976, Waddell was put on trial for the murder of Rachael Ross – and cleared. Waddell was defended by James Law, who had interesting links with Joe Beltrami. James Law and Joe Beltrami were both involved in the case of Maurice Swanson who was jailed for a bank robbery he did not commit, and received the first Royal Pardon of the century after some months in jail. Patrick Connolly Meehan was to be the next man to be pardoned.

The involvement of 'Tank' McGuinness was something of less than a surprise to Joe Beltrami. In his excellent book *A Deadly Innocence: The Meehan File,* Joe tells that in 1973 – with Meehan languishing in Peterhead with little prospect of freedom – McGuinness, a client, had told him several times that along with another man he was responsible for the murder of Rachael Ross.

This was bad news for Meehan because Joe Beltrami was adamant that solicitor/client confidentiality meant he could do nothing about it while McGuinness was alive. Meehan bitterly contested this view in later years but Joe has consistently defended his position as a working lawyer. And he wrote that such secret knowledge was a crushing burden for him to bear.

However, in March 1976 Tank McGuinness was found beaten and unconscious in Janefield Street, Parkhead. He died 13 days later in the Royal Infirmary without regaining consciousness. Joe Beltrami was now freed from his obligation, as he saw it, of silence. He was sure that McGuinness was the victim of a drunken brawl, but Ludovic Kennedy saw it differently and wrote in an English newspaper: 'The underworld killed the real Ayr murderer. It was only after his slaying that his solicitor, J Beltrami, was freed from his professional code of silence.' John 'Gypsy' Winning was the last person to be seen with Tank before his death. An underworld figure with a horrendous reputation, Winning was said to be McGuinness' closest 'friend'. He was eventually arrested in a pub in Gallowgate and charged with the murder. At the trial the indictment was withdrawn because of lack of evidence; Lord Wheatley instructed the jury to find him not guilty. But there was further mayhem on the way – Winning was himself murdered in a house in Fife in 1980. And Ian Waddell was also to meet a violent death at the hands of a 'friend'. Andrew Gentle was given two life sentences for murdering Waddell after the two of them had stabbed Josephine Chipperfield to death in a flat in Easterhouse. Lord Kincraig ordered him to serve not less than 20 years. Gentle himself was found dead in his cell in a Greenock prison in 1996. There were not thought to be suspicious circumstances. A dangerous man to the end, he had escaped twice when on escorted trips out of prison.

However, back in 1976 Paddy Meehan was on his way to freedom, though some remarkable disappointments still lay ahead. Seven years into his life sentence – almost all the time spent in solitary confinement – he was pardoned. Inevitably there was a wrangle about suitable financial compensation. The initial offer – not surprisingly rejected – was a miserly £7500, though years later it was increased to £50,000. In 1977 the then Scottish Secretary Bruce Millan ordered an inquiry by Lord Hunter into the whole affair. Who could have blamed Paddy Meehan if at last he felt he would be properly cleared? Five years and 500,000 words later, when the Hunter report was finally published – three months after Waddell's death – it was not to be. Lord Hunter said: 'The theory of an initial assault by Ian Waddell and Tank McGuinness, with a follow-up by Meehan and gunman Griffiths to open the safes believed to have been in the house, is a possibility that can't be ruled out.'

It was an incredible blow to Meehan and his supporters. The Edinburgh legal establishment was not going to completely exonerate Paddy. Ludovic Kennedy again took to the typewriter and in the *Sunday Standard* he was aggressively forthright. He made the point that Lord Hunter made it plain that McGuinness and Waddell, not Meehan and Griffiths, were the men who broke into the Ross bungalow and assaulted them. He claimed that it followed from this that Mr Ross' identification of Meehan's voice – such a feature of the actual trial all those years ago – was bogus. He went on to say that in his opinion the identification was almost certainly the result of the police tipping off Meehan's position in the line-up. Kennedy added: 'Why continue to bother about Meehan, you may ask (and I am always being asked) – a man who for so long was such a pest to society, and whom Lord Hunter has called, not without reason, a glib and inventive liar. There are two reasons. The first is that having served seven years, been granted a free pardon, and since gone straight, Meehan has fully discharged his debt to society. The second is that this case is now less about a person than about a principle. And that principle is that justice is, and should be, indivisible.' It was the fabled campaigner's opinion that the legal establishment continued to throw suspicion at Meehan to avoid further investigation of the claims of police planting evidence. Meehan's supporters were equally outraged in print and on the airwaves. Nicky Fairbairn, lawyer David Burnside and Ludovic Kennedy issued a statement saying that the suggestion that Mr Meehan had taken part in the crime in a manner never previously suggested was without any evidence. They also pointed out that in his terms of reference Lord Hunter, a High Court judge, had been expressly forbidden to comment on Meehan's guilt or innocence. Kennedy said: 'I think there is a feeling of disappointment and disbelief. Lord Hunter's report is really quite extraordinary, and coming from a High Court Judge, hard to credit.'

Meehan himself announced a new fight to clear his name. By now he was a legitimate businessman somewhat ironically selling security devices and double-glazing. And he was a well-kent figure in the *Herald* offices, then in Mitchell Street, enjoying frequent trips into town to chat with reporters in the newsroom or a nearby bar. From his Gorbals home he told reporters: 'I have to start all over again to clear my name.' And Bruce Millan, the Labour politician who had asked for the report, said that nothing in it had convinced him he was wrong to grant the free pardon. The allegations of police tampering with evidence were not going away either. David Scott, writing for the *Sunday Standard,* unearthed a series of intriguing reports pointing to police misbehaviour involving the grit found in Meehan's shoes and the slips of paper from the murder house found in Griffiths' car coat. Nicky Fairbairn, too, was hard-hitting in his criticism of the Hunter report. He pointed out that all the people who had fought for seven years to see justice done were criticised, while all the policemen who brought it about were absolved for their actions.

Politicians were now deeply involved and in December 1982 the Scottish Grand Committee discussed the Hunter report and its spin-offs. The committee heard accusations that the Ayrshire police had planted evidence against Meehan. These allegations resulted from a letter sent to Paisley Labour MP Allen Adams by a former assistant chief constable of Strathclyde, Arthur Bell. Mr Adams told the committee that the police in Ayrshire did plant some evidence according to Mr Bell, whom the MP regarded as a man of integrity and probably the cleverest detective in Glasgow. The committee also heard that the police had taken no action after Mr Ross had told them he had discovered that watches and rings had been stolen. Mr Adams said: 'There is little doubt that if these matters had been inquired into and reported to the Crown Office, there could have been other arrests.' Meehan could have been released or at least found not guilty or not proven.

Opening the debate, Mr Younger had said that Lord Hunter had been castigated – variously for imputing guilt to Mr Meehan, for not finding him innocent, and for not being able to conclude with certainty whether or not he had been involved in the crime. 'The fact is that Mr Meehan received a free pardon based on doubts about his conviction in October 1969 for murdering Mrs Ross. This fact is not affected by Lord Hunter's findings, which were directed at the performance of the authorities who investigated the murder.

'It has also been suggested that Lord Hunter exceeded his terms of reference in stating as a possibility that the crime at Ayr might have been the work of four men, including Mr Meehan, and further that this suggestion was quite unsupported by evidence.' Mr Younger claimed that Hunter's remit required him to examine the whole circumstances of the murder inquiry. Lord Hunter's comments flowed from his investigation of the role of the authorities involved, including accusations against the police. Far from being a breach of his terms of reference, this was an essential part of his remit. 'If this was a cover-up, I can't imagine what an exposé would have been like,' said Peter Fraser, the Solicitor General. This was followed by a pungent put-down. 'The truth,' answered John Maxton, the Labour MP for Cathcart.

According to *The Herald*, the debate could have been called a major victory for Meehan. MP after MP on all sides of the house recommended that the £7500 compensation awarded to him on his release should be increased. But after hearing the three-and-a-half-hour debate Paddy was still not satisfied. 'I want there to be no doubt that I was innocent of this crime, for which I spent seven years in solitary confinement,' he said. All the political talk had one solid result – the compensation became £50,000 (though at one time Joe Beltrami was looking for £100,000 for his client, a figure perhaps more appropriate for an innocent man who spent seven years in solitary). Money apart, it was all very unsatisfactory. Society was continuing to claim a high price from Paddy Meehan, still taunted by the Hunter report. He was now eking out a hard but legitimate existence in the security business.

But with the violent men of the Glasgow underworld who had been linked with the case all now dead, the saga was moving into a new stage – a mighty but bloodless war of words. Joe Beltrami had hit the bookshelves with considerable success with *A Deadly Innocence*, but some of the material in it had stoked the fires of a feud between Beltrami and Meehan. The response from Meehan was to publish his own side of the story in a book bizarrely published in Spain and called *Framed by MI5*. Joe Beltrami was quick to act, and the day after the book went on sale in Britain one of Glasgow's leading booksellers received a letter from Mr Beltrami's solicitors warning that Mr Meehan's version 'contained a considerable amount of libellous material'. The shop conceded that if allegations relating to Mr Beltrami were untrue, they could be sued. They issued a statement: 'While John Smith, as booksellers, are conscious of the inalienable right to the freedoms of speech and thought, there are perforce limitations on these freedoms. The facts set out in Mr Beltrami's book are, in many instances, inconsistent with those adumbrated by Mr Meehan. It is beyond doubt that Mr Meehan, a most singular and tenacious character, was wrongly convicted. It is equally beyond doubt that his story ought to be told, without let or hindrance.

'While the threat of libel action exists, Mr Meehan's story can not be given a full airing. It is John Smith's view that both books ought to be freely available, in order that the reading and interested public may make up their own minds to the truth or otherwise of the allegations of both authors.

'In the circumstances, John Smith's have decided to refuse to stock Mr Beltrami's book until he undertakes, in writing, not to sue John Smith's for selling allegedly libellous material.'

The Great Defender was unfazed. Noting that the bookshop's decision was disappointing, he added: 'That's their loss.'

Meehan wrote an article in *The Herald* on this literary stramash, and he did not mince his words. Writing of *A Deadly Innocence*, the safebreaker turned wordsmith said: 'I was somewhat surprised that he [Beltrami] now appears to accept that "with the benefit of hindsight" this "extremely strange case . . . could have stemmed from some kind of MI5 involvement."' In his own book – written after leaving Glasgow to settle close to family in Port Talbot – he claimed to have been the victim of an elaborate conspiracy, concocted by the security services, to keep him quiet over what he described as his role in the escape of the Soviet spy George Blake from a London prison in 1966. He even indulged his old passion for the truth drug. 'In closing, let me say how delighted I am to read in Beltrami's book that he is very much in favour of the use of the truth drug. Wouldn't it be interesting if he and I submitted ourselves to being questioned under the influence of the drug? The outcome would greatly assist the public in whether to go into any shop and buy Beltrami's *A Deadly Innocence* or stop me (when the police are not looking) in Glasgow's Argyle Street – or the Barras on a Sunday – and buy a copy of my *Framed by MI5*.'

His struggle to sell his book has left Glaswegians with a strangely sad memory of Meehan, a man tormented to the end and hawking his story on the city centre streets to anyone who would listen to him. He died of throat cancer in Swansea at the age of 67, in August 1994.

So ended one of the most remarkable stories in Scottish criminal history. Or did it? Is there still a twist left in this strange tale? A late revelation from one of the huge cast of characters involved – lawyers, politicians, and even the security services?

14

THE GUNRUNNER
WHO WALKED

Glaswegians are rightly fabled for their patter, the imaginative use of language. When it comes to crime there is something of a special vocabulary. 'To walk' might in some more refined city mean to take a stroll, to exercise gently. In Glasgow it means one thing – to stand trial and be cleared (or at least win a 'not proven' verdict!). The walking involved is down the courthouse steps into the nearest pub for some serious celebration with your 'connections'.

Perhaps the most famous Glasgow gangster to 'walk', in arguably the most fascinating of the city's big trials, was Paul Ferris. In March 1992 Ferris, then a baby-faced 28-year-old with the appearance of a successful young businessman, stood trial in Glasgow's High Court charged with killing Arthur Thompson Jnr and accused of six drugs and violence charges. The trial ran for 54 days and was the longest murder trial in Scottish criminal history: with unofficial estimates putting the cost at £750,000. More than 300 witnesses were cited for a trial said to have every ingredient – sex, drugs, humour, violence, love and tragedy. The charges against Ferris were:

1. The supply of heroin, cocaine, and ecstasy.
2. Attempting to murder Arthur Thompson Snr by repeatedly driving a motor car at him in May 1990.

3. Conspiring to assault John 'Jonah' McKenzie on 26 May 1991.
4. Shooting William Gillen in the legs and threatening to murder him.
5. Murdering Arthur Thompson Jnr in 1991 while acting with Robert Glover and Joseph Hanlon.
6. Illegal possession of a firearm.
7. Breach of the Bail Act.

Paul Ferris was found not guilty on all charges and emerged triumphant on the court steps, waving to photographers and ready to make the most sensational 'walk' of all.

Paul Ferris was born in Blackhill – described in one *Herald* report as a 'foul crime nursery on the north-east side of the city' – and embarked on an early life of villainy. Much was to happen before that bizarre appearance on the High Court steps. And much more after it, before Paul Ferris was jailed for ten years in July 1998 for his role in a major arms-dealing racket. The sentence handed down after a trial at the Old Bailey was later cut to seven years at an Appeal Court sitting in London in May 1999. Lord Justice Belden, sitting with Mr Justice Harrison and Mr Justice Lyas, reduced the sentence after making reference to a man who supplied huge quantities of guns to some of the UK's most vicious criminals. Registered gun dealer and former special constable Anthony Mitchell had admitted four firearms charges in which he supplied weapons to crooks, including Ferris. Mitchell was given eight years at the Old Bailey. Lord Justice Belden said: 'Bearing in mind the eight-year sentence given to this man, it is clear to us that the sentence imposed on Paul Ferris was too high.' All this was rather ironic, since in a leader at the conclusion of the trial *The Herald* had expressed the viewpoint that 'the vast majority of those to whom the name Paul Ferris means anything will be, frankly, disappointed that Judge Henry Blacksell was unable to send him down for 15 years. But tariffs are tariffs.' The leader went on to express the opinion that 'We are well pleased and relieved that Ferris, a ruthless professional criminal in Judge Blacksell's phrase, will be off the streets of Glasgow for at least six-and-a-half years.' The writer of the editorial then referred to the famous walk. 'Cleared of the charge of murdering Arthur 'Fat Boy' Thompson, the career gangster given the sobriquet Houdini is now in figurative chains but behind real bars where he belongs.'

But the story is getting ahead of itself. The downfall of Ferris may have been delayed after the Thompson trial, but there were plenty of other clues to his character. He seemed destined for notoriety. Indeed, in a TV documentary in 1995 he casually remarked: 'If anyone was born into crime, it was me. Crime is in my blood.' Long before the trial, events in the East End were demonstrating yet again what nonsense it was for Arthur Thompson Snr to carry on the ludicrous facade of being a retired businessman. Retired perhaps, but not from anything remotely resembling legitimate business. A full-scale turf war was going on for control of the network for the distribution of drugs and the huge profits that were at stake. The 'Fat Boy' was deeply involved in this struggle for power, but most newspaper accounts label him a loser from the start. By contrast, his father Arthur Snr had presence – anyone in his company could quickly scent a nasty mixture of power and danger. But young Arthur was overweight and had the fatal flaw of any gangster or gangster wannabee – he talked too much. His father may have ruled crime in Glasgow for years with only relatively short spells behind bars, but it was no surprise that young Arthur should at a relatively young age find himself doing 11 years for drug-dealing.

A fascinating background feature in *The Herald* at the end of the Ferris trial cast light on young Arthur's failings as a hard man. It told of a *Herald* reporter going north to Peterhead after the 1989 prison riots had subsided, and of a meeting with 'Fat Boy'. Most of those hard men involved in the riot had been moved to other places of incarceration but the young Thompson was still there. The reporter found him enjoying the feeling of having achieved some status merely by being there in a prison holding real men of violence and arch-troublemakers. But in reality his status was far from high with his fellow inmates. The idea behind this particular Press visit to the prison was to let prisoners have their say, in an enlightened reversal of previous prison policy that was held to be one of the sparks of the riots. Young Arthur delivered a wild-eyed rant on his innocence, on the corruption of the police, and of the complicity of the media which had landed him in jail. The report went on: 'As he raved on about getting justice he made one remark which underlined his craving for status. He referred to a previous visit by the then prisons director Mr Peter McKinlay, a well-known innovator, and said: "He left us on a bad downer. He did not seem to understand he was speaking to intelligent men, not a bunch of gas-meter bandits."' This was amusing, for young Arthur was looked on as little more than a gas-meter bandit by those around him. As the *Herald* reporter left the hall, a notorious murderer said out of the side of his mouth: 'That slavering bastard should shut up because he is safe in here. He will not survive a day outside.' It may not have been intended to be taken literally, but it was a belief echoed by other hard men in other jails.

This backgrounder, as they are known in newspapers, told of young Arthur continuing to try to wheel and deal from inside as he was moved through the prison system from one location to another – an inevitable part of the way things worked at that time. First he was moved to Shotts; then the would-be hard man – who was also known to the inmates as the Mars Bar Kid – was offered the chance to go to Dungavel but declined. An odd move, as at the time Shotts was tension-ridden and Dungavel was a semi-open prison in rural surroundings not far from Strathaven.

A second chance for a move came, this time to Noranside, described as a prison 'without wire or walls in the heart of rural Angus where Glasgow hard men are exposed to the civilising influence of agriculture'. Fat Boy was aware that he would qualify for his first home leave exactly six weeks after he entered

Noranside. A former governor who knew him well theorised that young Arthur had to take up his home leave, or after years spent boasting about resuming his drugs empire, lose face by staying in the relative safety of the prison. But that prophecy made back in Peterhead was about to come true: he didn't live through his first weekend outside. A man who knew him well told reporters: 'If he had had half a brain he could have taken over Glasgow's crime scene, including drugs. He was never sophisticated enough to get into the big time and everyone associated with him knew it.'

The end was sordid. Three shots punctured the night in Provanmill Road. Two .22 bullets went directly into his back; a third grazed his cheek. One bullet that entered through his back found its way to his heart. The Mars Bar Kid was still on his feet and there was no sign of blood, but he was mortally wounded. His sister Tracy heard the bangs and ran from her home hoping that the sounds were merely car backfires – not a promising line of reasoning in that area late at night! Her brother, arms outstretched, reportedly gasped: 'I've been shot, hen. I am going to collapse.' The time was 11.09 p.m. on 17 August 1991. There was a panic as Thompson was lifted into his brother's car and was driven at high speed to the Royal, where he died within the hour. Young Arthur was within a year of release when he was hit. The home visit had led to a meal in a city-centre Indian restaurant with his common-law wife Catherine. After the drive home he spent a few minutes in his parents' house but decided to walk the few yards to his own home and was gunned down before he could reach it.

And so it happened that some 14 weeks later, his one-time friend Paul John Ferris found himself charged with perhaps the most notorious gangland killing in a city that has seen plenty. Many of the 300 witnesses cited gloried in monikers that could have jumped off the pages of a Damon Runyon short story. Names bandied about in the blatts which Runyon might have noted included Brian 'Square Go' Graham, William 'the Rock' McLeod, 'Snazz' Adams, William 'Tootsie' Lobban, John 'Jonah' McKenzie,

William 'Gillie' Gillen and David 'Soagy' Logue. But this was no off-Broadway farce full of humour and homespun philosophy, a happy ending never far away. This was a story of drugs, gang warfare and ugly death on the streets. Nicknames were, however, an undeniable feature. Take one of the two shot dead in a car on the day of Fat Boy's funeral, Joe 'Bananas' Hanlon. Along with Bobby Glover he was killed in a well-timed gesture that would have won plaudits from a Mafia don. *The Herald* remarked that if Paul Ferris had a nickname, it was never mentioned in court – although one witness referred to him in court as 'Wee Paul'. In view of Mr Ferris' own status as a hard man – the genuine article, not the Thompson Jnr version – this might have been seen to be taking a risk.

Later in this saga Ferris, in London's top security Belmarsh Prison, was to take issue with an *Evening Times* report that he had been attacked by English geeks who were inside. *The Evening Times* was forced by lawyers to print a correction. It read: 'In our issue of 21 February 1998, we reported that Paul Ferris had been assaulted in Belmarsh Prison. This information came from a reliable source and was not denied by the prison authorities, but we now accept that there was no assault on Mr Ferris.' Status is important.

Back to Ferris' trial for the Arthur Thompson Jnr killing, a trial known as the best show in town during its lengthy run. It even featured badinage about chess between Lord McCluskey and Ferris himself. Apparently, the inmates of the segregation unit in Barlinnie are devoted to this age-old test of intellect, shouting the moves to each other. Paul Ferris added even more to his in-house prison status by reputedly winning £500 on a single move. According to the backgrounder, at one point Lord McCluskey became quite engrossed in a discussion on 'castling', a move which Ferris claimed he had been demonstrating to another prisoner. There was also the odd flash of humour: even Lord McCluskey found it hard to resist a smile on occasion. Once, on hearing that a witness had decided, in some haste, to go down the coast to Irvine on holiday without any luggage, he inquired incredulously: 'Didn't he bring a beach towel?'

Hundreds of thousands of words were spoken at the trial and it was all recorded verbatim by a team of around eight court shorthand writers. It is said that one *Herald* reporter filled 40 large notebooks. Among the productions in the mammoth trial were a bullet-proof vest, several firearms, ammunition and cartridge cases. The duration of the case was remarkable, a fact that was touched on by Donald Findlay QC at the end of yet another famously successful defence. He began an address to the jury: 'The seasons have come and gone, a General Election has been won and lost, according to your point of view, and Royal marriages have waxed and waned.' But behind the rhetoric lay what the trial judge Lord McCluskey called 'an extraordinary catalogue of lies, deceit, cruelty and death'. It exposed the struggle for control of the drug scene as a depravity far beyond the imagining of hard-working folk in the city's many douce suburbs. During the trial one man described two-and-a-half ounces of heroin as 'many happy days'. Another blamed indulging in drugs and drink for his amnesia over certain matters of concern to the court. And in a hark-back to the dark days of the ice-cream wars, there were admissions of vans being fire-bombed and allegations that they were used to sell drugs to children at street corners.

Many observers of the trial commented on how well turned-out many of the witnesses were and their ability to manage so well – with mobile phones and frequent holidays – on apparently meagre handouts from the taxpayers. However, according to *The Herald*, the most remarkable figure in the witness box was one Dennis David Woodman, whose abilities as a police informer in England had encouraged the authorities to create a new identity for him. However, Woodman was soon on the wrong side of the law in Scotland and ended up in Barlinnie, where he met up with Paul Ferris who was awaiting trial for shooting William Gillen in the legs. Woodman claimed that in snatched conversations between the exercise cage and the cells Ferris had confessed to the shooting of Arthur Thompson Jnr. Some witnesses said that such conversations were possible; others said not. Woodman gave evidence lasting 19 hours and 50 minutes. He showed flashes of temper when questioned by Donald Findlay, even making sneering remarks about the Rangers football team to the lawyer and super-fan. Paul Ferris denied having conversations with Woodman and dismissed him as 'no competition'. Lord McCluskey had given Woodman much rope and tolerated his frequent bad behaviour, but he eventually warned him about this, saying he had allowed him to act as he did to show what kind of person he was. This new ploy subdued Woodman in his later evidence. And his credibility was destroyed when his claim that his two children had been killed in a car crash was proved to be false. The truth that they were alive came out by accident in a question to his half-brother.

This most remarkable of trials came to a close when on Thursday, 11 June 1992 the jury retired to consider a verdict. They spent the night in hotels and returned on the Friday afternoon at 3.30 p.m. Paul Ferris was smartly dressed, as he had been throughout the trial, as he listened to the clerk ask the spokesman for the jury if they had agreed on their verdicts. He replied quietly: 'Yes'. He then answered, 'Not guilty by a majority', as he was asked the verdicts on the first four charges. Tension rose as the gallery awaited the verdict on the fifth charge – that of murdering Arthur Thompson Jnr. There was a cry of delight and muffled applause as the spokesman announced a unanimous not guilty. In the end all the charges were thrown out. The court reports tell of Donald Findlay turning backwards in his seat to congratulate Paul Ferris, now looking visibly drained.

Lord McCluskey told Ferris he was free to go and thanked the jury for their services. He went on to say that it was not the practice in Scotland for the judge to comment in any way on the judgement of the jury, but it was plain that in relation to the murder charge 'you have wholly rejected the evidence of

Woodman'. He said that in doing this they had also rejected allegations made against a solicitor representing Ferris. Woodman claimed he had been offered a bribe by this solicitor. The scene was set for the walk down the courtroom steps. There, Ferris was asked if he would now be in fear of his life. He replied: 'Not at all. Mr Woodman put me in this position.' He went on to say that he now intended to enjoy himself and remarked that a public inquiry into the activities of Woodman would be in order for the benefit of justice.

Clearly, the comprehensive dismissal of Woodman's tales played a large part in the clearing of Ferris, but there were other important factors – particularly with regard to the shooting of William Gillen. Donald Findlay made much of what he called 'the failure of the Crown to call a key witness', one Thomas McGraw. McGraw was alleged to be the instigator of William Gillen being shot in the legs in a lay-by on the Glasgow-Kilmarnock road. But Mr McGraw had not given evidence, he told the jury. He said Mr Gillen had claimed that Mr McGraw was there on the night of the shooting and that he had ordered it. He went on: 'McGraw was supposed to be a participant and he is Crown witness no 214 – and yet the Crown never called him. If you leave a gap like that, it is too much to ask you to ignore it.'

This trial also provided one last chance for Arthur Thompson Snr to grab the limelight and yet again deny that he was a Godfather. In the witness box he was asked directly if he was a criminal overlord in Glasgow. He claimed that such allegations were nonsense and made the grim joke that he would have to stuff his mouth with cotton wool and speak like Don Corleone. He claimed his son had nothing to do with drugs and that the heroin conviction was a police fit-up. Asked if his son's murder could have anything to do with the drugs trade in Glasgow, his answer was: 'Nothing at all'. The court was told that he received £93 a week in invalidity benefit as a result of a gunshot wound caused by one of the attempts on his life over the years. He vehemently rejected any suggestion that he had orchestrated the murders of Bobby Glover and Joe 'Bananas' Hanlon. And he was not impressed by the pomp of the High Court, at one point imperiously instructing the advocate depute to 'wait till I finish'. Nothing if not consistent, old Arthur was at his best when a letter from Woodman was read out referring to him as the Godfather of Glasgow who worked for the Kray twins. Mr Findlay asked, 'This letter is painting a picture of you as a major criminal. Can you think of any reason why a man you don't know and have never met should say he is on your side?' 'The man is a nut. He wanted this letter to come here as a production,' he replied defiantly.

If all that is not amusing enough, the *Herald's* much-lauded Diary found something to laugh at in a collection of what were described as 'wee stories that kept up the spirits of the legal eagles and the journos during the 54 days of the trial'. First was a tale of how a common-law widow – if there is such a thing – of one of the gangland victims proved a formidable witness. She was asked if her man was of regular habits. She snapped: 'His tea was oan the table at five. If he wisnae there he didn't get it.' Asked if he had any other girlfriends, she smiled grimly. 'He had one once.' Pause. 'Why? Are ye gonnie surprise me?' A witness poured scorn on the evidence of this man's 'long-term' friend, a Miss X. Paul Ferris said: 'He was a big brave boy – but no way would he have parked with Miss X outside his girlfriend's house. First, she would have beaten him up. Then she would have beaten up Miss X. Then she would have beaten up the car.'

Another jest was at the expense of an individual said not to be the most reliable of hitmen. After being given a £500 advance and a sawn-off shotgun, and told the names of two or three Duke Street pubs his target regularly visited, he conspicuously failed to encounter his victim. He hid his weapon under some bricks at Hogganfield Loch but, fearing the wet weather would make it go rusty, he retrieved the gun and sold it to a scrap dealer. And according to the Diary, the spirit of the malaprop lived on in the trial. Describing a woman who had given evidence, a witness said that she was an alcoholic and 'at the time she spoke to the polis she wasn't compos mental'. The Diary awarded what it called the Most Abrupt Change of Evidence Award to a hardened criminal who described a fellow villain as: 'Not a very nice person.' Asked for clarification he replied: 'He's a f****** toerag!'

The trial may have ended, leaving Ferris to enjoy the status bestowed on him by the criminal fraternity for the most famous 'walk' in Glasgow, but it was business as usual for the police trying to control the turf wars of the East End. Paul Ferris had not killed Arthur Thompson Jnr, but Hanlon and Glover were dead and no-one was any the wiser about who killed them. The early favourite theory was that they were taken out in revenge for young Arthur's dramatic demise. Even a year after their deaths many aspects of the double killing were being investigated. And a more subtle theory had emerged – they were killed by their own associates in an effort to patch up relations with Arthur Jnr's connections. The duo were well known to the police. Glover had been given bail shortly before the murder, after an incident in which a man was knee-capped. Hanlon was reputed to be the strong-arm man for the drug runners known as the Barlanark Team. Not for the first time in the East End, a wall of silence was encountered by the investigators. Fear helped make it one of Glasgow's most enduring murder mysteries.

Not long after this sensational trial old Arthur succumbed to a heart attack, an ironically normal end for a man steeped in violence who had survived three gangland assassination attempts. The news moved Paul Ferris – aka 'Baby Face', 'Houdini' or 'Wee Paul' – into Mafia Don mode. He claimed he wanted to make peace with the Thompsons. He told reporters: 'My one regret is not having spoken to him. I did try to do so after the trial but a meeting could not be set up. I really did not get the opportunity to clear things up – and I will not now.' In fact, in the earlier years Ferris was said to have been treated like a member of the family by old Arthur.

And for a while he was close to young Arthur. He had been brought up near the Thompson home in Blackhill and had at one time worked in the old man's garage. Later he claimed to make a living as a car salesman and by dabbling in double-glazing. Before he fell out with young Arthur, Ferris often visited him in prison.

And Ferris was still making headlines – in England as well as Scotland now. In a trial in 1993 he was accused of being the mastermind behind a failed bank robbery in Devon – although he was never tried for the offence. Six Glaswegians were given lengthy sentences and the readers of the English newspapers were given some eye-opening insights into crime in Glasgow. During the trial the jury was told lurid tales of merciless tactics employed in Glasgow's gangland. These included cold-blooded executions with the victims shot in the buttocks and then in the back of the head. Other ploys included threatening elderly relatives of enemies and gunpoint confrontations with anyone trying to move in on the scene. There were also claims that 'leggy blondes' were paid to wine, dine and seduce enemies who didn't know that the women had been infected with the Aids virus. The reference to shootings in the buttocks adds conviction to claims that in the late '90s the habit of putting a bullet up the anus of dead victims as a sort of signature had become known as the 'Glasgow goodbye'.

The next year Ferris was in court in England, when he was fined £250 for possessing cocaine and cannabis. His lawyer told magistrates in Salford, Greater Manchester, that he took cocaine to ease a skin problem. His hotel room had been raided as a result of a tip-off. He was described as a second-hand car salesman in court and admitted the possession. Always good for a quote outside a court room – guilty or innocent – he said: 'My skin condition is brought on by stress and the drug helps me to relax. But I am not a habitual user of the stuff.' He then got into a friend's Jaguar and added: 'I am no gangster. The last gangster in Scotland was Arthur Thompson.' This minor court appearance and a few other clashes with the law were a mere prelude to Ferris' next big trial – and a downfall that sent him into Belmarsh high-security prison for a long stretch. 'Helmarsh', as the English criminal fraternity like to call it, was also at the time of writing home to Ronnie Biggs and Jeffrey Archer – a big-time pad for a violent career criminal from one of Glasgow's toughest schemes.

But before his appearance in the Old Bailey, Ferris had a spectacular and controversial TV appearance which shed some light on his character. He was interviewed by John McVicar – once described as Britain's most wanted man, but in 1995 a journalist and broadcaster. Ferris claimed that the programme gave him the opportunity to come to terms with his life and set the record straight. In the style of his old East End mentor Arthur Thompson, he described himself as a 'reformed criminal'. He claimed he was being demonised in the eyes of the public, and admitted that he believes he will die a violent death. In a preview of the programme he said he had been asked if he believed that he would end up on a mortuary slab. With the cheek of old Arthur he said: 'I think everyone ends up there some day but my biggest fear is I will be put there by the police.' One of the *Herald's* showbiz team watched the film and remarked, 'Paul John Ferris is most certainly a frighteningly violent young man. And the chilling thing about him when you see him on a television screen is the fact that he is not chilling. At least not to look at. He appears ordinary; you would pass him on the street without a second glance. And that is probably just as well, for a second glance might bring you to his attention. And you do not want to be drawn to the attention of Paul John Ferris.' He went on to describe the programme as genuinely shocking and say that in it, Ferris claims that he is neither a bully nor a gangster. And then Ferris adds: 'But that doesn't mean you have got to let people stand on your toes. If they do that you have got to jump on their neck and break it.' 'Wee Paul' went on to talk about his life in the East End. 'I've always used a weapon of sorts,' he says, 'whether it be a baseball bat or a knife.' He also discussed his early days as a collector of 'dues' for Arthur Thompson.

This was followed the next year with an intriguing attack on Ferris by, of all people, Bobby Glover's mother. She slammed him for placing an advert in the *Evening Times* to mark the fifth anniversary of Glover's death outside the Cottage Bar. Kathy Glover stormed: 'This is the kind of tribute we can do without. Robert would be alive today if it wasn't for people like Paul Ferris.' She added, 'I have never liked Paul Ferris. Why has he never stood on my floor if he was such a friend of my son's? I knew nothing about my son's life but I knew he was up to no good. I always let him know I loved him as a son but didn't like what he did.' But Paul Ferris responded in what seemed like his familiar Mafia Godfather mode. 'I think I am speaking on behalf of both families. It is a time when both want to get on with their lives. The wives in particular have a new life ahead of them. I think the female members of the families want to put this behind them. The memorial was placed as a public recognition that it was a bad time of year for his friends as well. Every year the number of tributes gets less and less.' Don Corleone couldn't have put it better.

With the once almighty Thompson empire in ruins after the death of both old and young Arthurs, Paul Ferris was not the only name in the frame as the neds fought over the pickings left by the cutting-down of the family. In July 2000 *The Herald* looked at the career of Thomas McGraw, a name which features frequently in the archive. It was said that he was known as the 'Licensee' and was a candidate for the role of Glasgow's new Godfather. He was said to be a member of the notorious Barlanark Team and to have built a multi-million-pound fortune on the wreckage of the Thompson empire. Tam McGraw was apparently given the sobriquet of Licensee when he bought the infamous Caravel Bar in Barlanark, although his wife was the owner. The Caravel was something of an East End legend. It was over the years a drinking howff for many an underworld name, and the police believe that much thuggery and lawbreaking was discussed across the bar by some customers. Recently there was legal squabbling over the development of the site, but the bar itself was bulldozed in mysterious circumstances after underworld informers suggested to the police that it had played a role in the deaths of Joe 'Bananas' Hanlon and Bobby Glover. But any notion of a forensic examination of the premises in a search for clues was ruled out by the demolition.

However, McGraw was to feature in another famous Glasgow 'walk'. And like Ferris, his defence counsel was none other than Donald Findlay QC. In July 1988 Thomas McGraw, alleged to have bankrolled a major drug-running operation, walked free after the jury returned a majority 'not proven' verdict after a lengthy 55-day trial. *The Herald's* law correspondent reported that Mr McGraw's release came after a masterful performance by Donald Findlay, who described the accused as an Arthur Daley figure, 'ducking and diving'. Asked for a comment when he left the High Court in Edinburgh, McGraw told reporters to 'f*** off' before being driven off in a black Mercedes.

McGraw's brother-in-law was jailed for 10 years for his part in the cannabis-smuggling operation; Graeme Mason – nicknamed Del Boy – was sentenced to eight years, and Paul Flynn six. This was one of Scotland's longest running and most expensive drug trials and at the end Lord Bonomy paid tribute to the 'dignity and diligence' of the jury. The *Herald* report rather acerbically pointed out that, in what could be interpreted as a criticism of the way the Crown case was presented, the judge also praised the jury for the considerable care they had taken in considering the 'welter of evidence which emerged in a fairly disjointed fashion as the trial proceeded'. Taking into account legal fees, the long-running investigations and the high security police operation which surrounded the case, the trial is estimated to have cost £2 million.

The Herald considered the result a disappointment for the police and prosecution authorities – only three men left in the dock out of an original 11. But for Donald Findlay there was only one word

– triumph. The court report said: 'In a masterful speech to the jury, he hammered home the point that the case against his client was flimsy and that there was not one scrap of evidence to show Mr McGraw's money was going to Spain to buy the drugs.' The judge told the three convicted men: 'The jury have found you guilty of playing various roles in what was a major drug importation operation which has been a disturbing example of organised crime in the midst of needy Glasgow communities.' Donald Findlay painted a very different picture of Thomas McGraw's business activities, explaining to the jury that he was a bit of an Arthur Daley – 'doing a bit of this and a bit of that' and not paying income tax or VAT. He told the court that coupled with his legitimate business activities, his client's objection to paying tax explained why he was in possession of huge sums of money. His cash came from a cash-and-carry business, ice-cream vans, and the Caravel public house.

It was said that at one point the taxman had caught up with him and he had been forced to hand over £100,000. Even then he was left with more than £300,000 of legitimate money. While evasion of tax was not an enviable quality, it did not make McGraw a drug smuggler. Donald Findlay went on: 'There is not a single scrap of evidence in this case which in any way connects Thomas McGraw with the bus [the conduit for the drugs, it was alleged], holidays in Spain or anything else.' He warned the jury that the Crown case was based on suspicion and possibilities, and that had never been enough to convict someone of a crime in Scotland. If ever there was a case of the Crown adding two and two and coming up with seven-and-a-half this was it. So Thomas McGraw – who has always denied wrongdoing – left court a free man. The next time he featured strongly in the files was in a report in March 2000 that he was selling his business empire – including a car-hire company alleged to have been the centre of a police and customs operation over allegations of the laundering of drugs money – to settle in Tenerife where he owns property.

Back in Britain, Paul Ferris was heading for a day in court from which there was to be no escape. This time the clang of a cell door was to remain with him for a long time. In July 1998 he was found guilty of masterminding a shipment of guns and explosives. The police believed that cracking this case had prevented a major crime-war in Scotland – though *The Herald* thought it was much more likely that the weapons had been intended for Manchester, where sub-machine guns were said to be a designer accessory for drug-dealers. Ferris was posing as a respectable security expert when he was caught red-handed after a massive two-year surveillance operation by detectives working for what is known as the National Crime Squad. They seized sub-machine guns, ammunition and explosives that had been bought by Ferris.

For a career criminal who had jousted with the forces of law and order over the years, often with success, his downfall contained elements of farce. One night, on a London to Glasgow sleeper train, a Glaswegian who was blind drunk and being abusive to other passengers caught the attention of the Transport Police. They boarded the train when it pulled into Preston Station. Any notion that this was a simple case of a bevvied-up, obnoxious Glaswegian causing trouble soon exploded. The drunk was Joe McAulay, a security worker who was a trusted foot soldier for Paul Ferris. When the police on the train opened his holdall they got the shock of their lives. Inside was a .22 Ceska handgun, a silencer and rounds of ammunition. As McAulay languished in a cell in Preston, the phone lines buzzed with frantic calls from Ferris, who was staying in Surrey with a close friend called Henry Suttee. Ferris later told the police that his calls to McAulay were to let him know of progress he was making in getting hold of that year's hot toy, a Buzz Lightyear doll featured in the movie *Toy Story*. He also told police that he thought McAulay had got a gun to deal with someone who was 'hassling' his teenage daughter.

But the drunken escapade of his associate was to cost 'Houdini' dear. This time there was no escape. A senior crime-squad officer who helped put Ferris away told the *Evening Times*: 'The link with McAulay was vital. It showed us there was a system going on.' Police believed that McAulay was sent to London by Ferris. He flew down and bought the pistol from gun-supplier John Ackerman. Aware of the danger posed by security at Gatwick, he decided to take the train home. In Preston Crown Court he admitted that the weapon – fitted with a silencer – and 39 rounds of ammunition in his luggage were intended to cause 'fear or violence'. The judge said he was plainly carrying the gun for someone else.

McAulay's trial was merely a trailer for the big show at the Old Bailey. There, on England's most famous criminal stage, justice finally caught up big-time with the baby-faced hoodlum from the slums of Glasgow's East End. Ferris was convicted of trafficking in sub-machine guns and explosives. Judge Henry Blacksell told Ferris he had 'arranged, paid for and taken delivery of a lethal parcel of weapons'. He hardly dared to speculate, he said, on the potential for death and destruction they might have caused had they reached their intended criminal destination. 'I have no doubt you are a dangerous and ruthless professional criminal. Those who choose to deal in such arms can only expect prison sentences of great length.'

There was a certain symmetry in the fact that Glasgow officers were present when armed surveillance teams swooped on Ferris and his accomplices. The police had followed the gang as their Nissan Prairie headed north through London's West End. The judge acknowledged that the destination of the guns was not known, and a senior police source indicated to *The Herald* that the weapons – three 9 mm Ingram Mac 10 sub-machine guns capable of firing 1100 rounds a minute – 'had very limited application to the Scottish drug scene.' *The Herald* attributed the success of the operation to intelligence from Strathclyde police; they kept a close eye on Ferris, whom they regarded as a cruel and ruthless enforcer who had worked for two major criminal empires in the past two decades. Henry Suttee was also jailed and John Ackerman pleaded guilty to his part in the gunrunning conspiracy. One of the English detectives involved, Chief Inspector Peter Spindler, underlined the seriousness of the case: 'If these military weapons, capable of emptying a 25-round magazine in two seconds, had found their way into the hands of the criminal underworld, the consequences could have been devastating.' Paul Ferris had graduated a long way from the baseball bat.

The court heard that the Glasgow hard man had used everything he could to divert attention from his activities. A 28-year-old woman, Constance Howarth, was used to transport the box of guns and explosives he had purchased from Ackerman in her battered Vauxhall Nova. Armed police officers watched as she drove off, and when she was stopped at lights on the A1 she was surrounded by officers screaming 'we are armed'. Bundled out of the car she protested, 'I'm just a girl. Me, I don't know anything about guns.' She blamed a boyfriend, since disappeared, for setting her up to do his dirty work and branded him a 'rat'. Ferris and Suttee were arrested on the same day. Not unexpectedly Ferris had a twist in the story to tell in court. He said he was involved in criminal activity when he visited Ackerman, but it was not gunrunning. He claimed he thought he was getting a box full of counterfeit bank notes and printing plates. He accused Ackerman of tricking him by putting guns and explosives in the box. But this was a fantasy that wouldn't wash. In the prosecution's final speech it was said that the defendant's claims of innocence had a 'hollow ring' to them. He had been caught red-handed and was trying to lie his way out of trouble.

Some of the lies were causing ripples 400 miles to the north. Ferris' tales of using a Chinese passport scam as cover had Glasgow's Chinese underworld in a fury. During his evidence he claimed he was in London as part of a ploy to provide passports for illegal immigrants. But Oriental crime bosses told the *Evening Times* that Ferris had nothing to do with them and they resented him bringing up their shady deals in court. And in the end the lies and obfuscation failed. Ferris was, in the words of that splendid *Herald* leader, nailed at last.

Nailed, at least temporarily, he may have been but there was yet another twist left in the Paul Ferris saga. In the spring of 2002 news came that he was about to be released on parole after serving more than half his seven-year sentence. The word was that this time he had learned a lesson; the baby faced so-called 'crime lord' was pledged to turn over a spectacular new leaf.

As the gates of high security Frankland Prison in Durham clanged behind him he was, as ever, in his business man mode of dark blue suit, white shirt and blue tie. And before his release he issued a statement: 'There is just one option when I get out – to go straight. My plan is to become a decent loving father, to provide my family with security, free from a life of crime. No doubt I have enemies, including some rogue police and their criminal partners. They'd love something unsavoury to happen to me.'

Part of the new life plan was to become a man of letters. While in prison he had co-authored a book called *The Ferris Conspiracy* which dripped blood from its pages and sold well in crime-conscious Glasgow. The next step was aimed higher up the literary ladder; this time it was to be a novel no less. But *Deadly Divisions* – which had some incidents perhaps based on real life – was not to achieve critical acclaim. Far from it. The reviews were mostly negative.

But in a headline provoking new twist in the saga it was not long before Paul Ferris was back in Frankland Prison for allegedly breaching his parole conditions. And there were further shocks to come for Glaswegians who had for some years been overdosing on café lattes in the city's trendy watering holes, and developing a growing complacency about the gangs. One spring morning their attention was snatched from the welter of the arts reviews that pass for features these days by a startling piece of real news. Tam McGraw, who featured earlier in this chapter, was allegedly attacked in the street and, apparently, saved from serious injury by a bullet-proof vest. Knives were said to have been involved.

There was simmering tension on the streets this violent spring-time which saw another broad daylight attack. This time on TC Campbell as he awaited the appeal hearing on his conviction for his part in the killing of the Doyles in the Ice Cream Wars.

A feature of this new violence was the use of golf clubs as weapons. A set of clubs in the boot would not normally attract police attention and a whack over the head with a five iron could not be taken lightly. Nevertheless it was reported that TC was feeling 'brand new' on his release from hospital. He talked of being attacked by two men – one with a golf club – and said there was murderous intent.

A few weeks later, in mid-June, Paul Ferris was again the main man in the headlines. He was released from prison in England and taken back to Glasgow by friends. It was said that he had been told there were no grounds for him being in prison.

The happenings of this violent spring were a warning that, as in every city, there were still factions ready to fight. But for once the authorities took their heads out of the sand and introduced a touch of realism. Charles Gordon, leader of Glasgow City Council, dismissed talk of a return to the 'No Mean City' image as an exaggeration. He saw it as a periodic eruption of gang warfare and said, 'While I obviously deplore the negative aspect it is having on the city, I don't think ordinary Glaswegians or people visiting the city should be put off. Glasgow is no different from every big city in the world.' Amen to that.

15

IN THE FOOTSTEPS
OF 'THE CAPTAIN'

Sir Percy Sillitoe was an innovative and intelligent policeman – as his early use of radio cars showed – as well as brick-hard in his determination to clear the streets of the pre-war razor men and bicycle-chain wielders. The man nicknamed 'The Captain' by his men was an exceptional chief constable, a truly hard act to follow. Such was the public perception of him that, to this day, the mention of Glasgow gangs makes people remember his name. He was the first in a succession of high-profile chief constables who led the fight against crime in the city. Many years span his stewardship of the forces of law and order to that of the new man at the helm, Willie Rae, who took on the top police job in Scotland in July 2001. With local government reorganisation, the City of Glasgow Police of proud legend gave way to the Strathclyde Police. The patch had got bigger, but despite successes down the years, problems remain. No one who takes on the leadership of such a force can expect an easy ride – from the public, the Press or the villains themselves.

Willie Rae faced tough competition: other candidates included the deputy chief constable of Greater Manchester and the deputy chief constable of the Royal Ulster Constabulary. A senior police source told the *Evening Times* that nine people asked for information packs about the job, but on receiving them four did not apply because: 'Many of the people holding chief and deputy chief constable jobs down south and in Scotland are of the opinion that

Strathclyde is too big a job for them to handle. It will also be difficult to follow in the footsteps of John Orr [the retiring Chief].' The list of famous names who have led the force is indeed impressive: among them Sir David McNee, the late Sir Patrick Hamill, Sir Andrew Sloan, Sir Leslie Sharp and John Orr, who took over in 1996. But Willie Rae has the big advantage of knowing the force well. He was originally with Dunbartonshire Constabulary but began to work in Glasgow and its surroundings in 1975 when the two forces were merged. He worked his way up through the ranks, holding a number of leading roles in specialised departments before becoming an assistant chief constable. In this role he was responsible for personnel matters.

He left Strathclyde to become chief constable of Dumfries and Galloway in September 1996. He became president of the Association of Chief Police Officers in Scotland in July 2001. Willie Rae knows he faces a tough job and is well aware that the face of crime has changed in many ways, even since he joined the force. Gangs remain but in different forms, and even the forces that drive petty crime like muggings and housebreaking have changed. Much of the trouble revolves round one word – drugs. Willie Rae gave a good example of this in an interview with the *Evening Times* shortly before he took over. With barely a foot back in the door of the Pitt Street HQ he talked of drugs as one of the biggest problems for his force. He has his own experience of how policing has changed since he joined the force. He started as a cadet straight from school at 15 and recalls: 'I was a very active young policeman and I caught a lot of criminals in my life as a constable and a sergeant in the first 12 years of my service, but I never once caught a drugs offender. Drunkenness was the main problem I dealt with on the streets.'

When he came back to Glasgow after serving with considerable success in the south of Scotland, he left his old patch with the lowest recorded level of reported crime since 1989. But Dumfries and Galloway was no parochial posting, and when in charge there he led the organisation of the Lockerbie bombing trial in the Netherlands – a task which involved investigations in 70 countries. There was some irony in the fact that the smallest force in the UK was called on to police the largest mass-murder trial in the history of the Scottish judicial process. The Lockerbie connection saw him travelling to Capitol Hill in Washington for a ceremony praising the people of the town and Dumfries and Galloway for their role in the aftermath of the appalling tragedy, which claimed 270 lives in 1988 when a Pan Am clipper, en route to America, was blown out of the sky.

But even in the leafy rural surrounds of Dumfries and Galloway, Willie Rae was not remote from the drug problem. He told his interviewer that even there, there is not a corner unaffected by drugs. One of the solutions to the problem that blights communities throughout Scotland, rural and urban, is – according to Willie Rae – raising awareness. 'There is a surprising number of people out there who feel that because of their lifestyle it will never come to their door . . . People must communicate with their children who often know more about drugs than they do.'

Willie Rae was also frank about other changes in policing. You suspect that the brute force employed by Percy Sillitoe, while arguably appropriate for the time, needs some moderation in the 21st century. Willie Rae's early experiences in the force shaped him and his attitude to policing. And he talks of images of routine and regular domestic violence that will live with him forever. 'Something that shocked me was the level of violence towards women in a domestic setting. I have never forgotten when I first heard a woman with a broken nose say, "I know I deserved a hammering, but he didn't have to do this to me." Somehow she felt her partner had a right to beat her up every Friday or Saturday night.' He has tried to be as supportive as possible to organisations like Women's Aid. 'It is something I am passionate about. I think it is absolutely despicable that in our modern society we still have this type of crime in such prevalence in our communities.'

At 51 Willie Rae is raring to go. And you feel that policing in Strathclyde continues in good hands. Certainly, there is continuity – for before he left in 1996 he had worked closely with five chief constable predecessors. The force he inherits has a remarkable history. In July 2000 the *Evening Times* reported that the roots of policing in Glasgow stretch back even before 1829, when Sir Robert Peel was given the credit for starting the first modern-day police service. But Alastair Dinsmore, chairman of the Glasgow Police Heritage Society (Honorary President Sir David McNee), told the *Evening Times*: 'Most history books credit Peel with the founding of modern policing in 1829. But for some reason historians in England have ignored the fact that Glasgow's police were established under the Glasgow Police Act of 1800 – fully 29 years beforehand. . . . It'd be nice to see the credit go where it belongs. All we want to do is to set the record straight.'

Mr Dinsmore was a police inspector who took early retirement and became the deputy curator of Glasgow's fabled police black museum. No other Scottish police force has dealt with so many high-profile cases, many of them chronicled in this book. *The Evening Times* report remarked that, amazingly, it was as long ago as 1788 – the year before the French revolution – that a handful of far-sighted Glasgow magistrates looked at community policing. Up till then the citizens, around 40,000 at the time, were under the protection of a combination of watchmen and the city guard which was made up of ordinary townspeople. 'Basically,' said Alastair, 'people tended to stay in after dark, and with good reason. The only ones who ventured out were ladies of the night and such like. There was a lot of poverty and, of course, when you get poverty there is a lot of crime.' For the criminals who got caught, the punishment could be severe. You could be sent to the gallows for theft or forgery. An alternative to the death sentence could be transportation to a penal settlement in Australia – the six-month journey by sea in a prison vessel was so harsh that for some the death sentence might have been preferable.

The start of organised policing arrived in 1788, with the appointment of an inspector and a handful of officers. This pace-setting operation was short-lived before cash ran out. (Shortage of money and conflict between council and police on resources was still evident at the end of the 20th century!) The city fathers realised that the answer was an Act of Parliament to levy rates to finance the police force. But in 1788, magistrates put together proposals for a force to prevent crime before it happened. 'This approach had not been done before – as far as we know – anywhere in the UK,' said Alastair. 'They thought up the idea of a municipal police force controlled by commissioners elected from tradespeople and merchants.

'The list of duties they came up with would fit easily into today's police function. The police would have a uniform and swear an oath. They would patrol the streets in shifts for 24 hours. They would deter thieves by concentrating on the receivers of stolen property – without the people to buy stolen goods, the market for the thief would be diminished, the same as today.

'They would keep an eye on taverns, where criminals hung out, and create a book containing information on all the criminals they dealt with – an early form of intelligence.' The *Evening Times* reporter found this amazing, groundbreaking stuff and described reading much similar stuff in the handwritten minutes of the early force in the Mitchell Library. However, the early start of policing was not without its problems. The minutes recorded that in 1789 a Master of Police was appointed with eight constables under him, but after a year lack of money again killed off the enterprise.

The Napoleonic Wars got in the way and it took 12 years for the Act of Parliament to be enacted. The fact that the Act was for the benefit of far-away Glasgow didn't help, either. 'Most of the people in power weren't too worried about what was happening in Glasgow,' said Alastair Dinsmore. 'Plus the rich merchants in London didn't want mere commoners having power over them and did everything they could to prevent policing in the capital.'

As with much in the development of Glasgow, the tobacco barons had a hand in the founding of the police. Patrick Colquhoun, who had been Lord Provost and responsible for the city's Chamber of Commerce, moved down south as a magistrate in 1789 and saw how bad the policing – or lack of it – was there. Six years later he wrote a book on how the London police could be improved. He had seen the Glasgow experiment at first hand and used these ideas in his own plans for a London force.

All this inspired the setting-up of the Thames River Police and the Metropolitan Force in London in 1829. But there is little denying Glasgow's claim to have been at the cutting edge of city policing in Britain.

The Police Museum itself is a splendid tribute to more than 200 years of crime-fighting. Among the many cases featured is that of Jessie McLachlan, who was sentenced to death after killing a servant with an iron cleaver in a house in wealthy Sandyford Place in the summer of 1862. During the investigation of the crime a smart medical man got her to leave her bloody footprint on a piece of wood. And it matched a bloody footprint found on the actual site of the crime. The wicked Jessie was fortunate that her sentence was commuted to life in jail. The block of bloodstained wood is just one of many fascinating exhibits in the museum featuring the city's history of crime.

No doubt Willie Rae will feature strongly in any future tales of battles against the hard men: you can't be a chief constable in Glasgow without some guaranteed tribulation. One chief who was linked with many of the most infamous names was Sir James Robertson who died in 1990 aged 84. His time at the top took in the rampage of James Griffiths, the violent gunman from Rochdale who was shot down in Springburn after the dramatic – and rare – order to draw arms was given. And, of course, he was involved in dealing with the Meehan case, the exploits of Tank McGuinness, Ian Waddell and Bible John.

The veteran detective involved in the Bible John investigations,

Joe Beattie, said on Sir James' death: 'I can't say a bad word about him. He was a gentleman through and through. Sometimes I thought he was too nice to be a chief constable. He was too humane!' But Sir James is probably best remembered as the Chief who introduced his Untouchables to the streets of Glasgow. This was a group of plain-clothes officers with a free-ranging role to cut crime on the streets. Chief Robertson had a lifelong interest in the welfare of youth, a real priority in the deprived areas of Glasgow and naturally he was deeply involved in the Easterhouse Project so beloved of entertainer Frankie Vaughan and chronicled elsewhere in this book.

Sir James retired as chief of the old city of Glasgow force in 1971 and was succeeded by Sir David NcNee, who went on to become perhaps the most distinguished of all Scottish police chiefs and commissioner of the Metropolitan Police in London, serving from 1977 to 1982. Nicknamed 'the Hammer', McNee was a particularly effective leader of big-city police forces and like Sillitoe, inventive and forward-looking. His influence over policing in Glasgow was and is enormous. Bill Robertson, an assistant chief constable in Glasgow and Cleveland in the early '90s, made some interesting remarks to *The Herald*. 'Some police officers think their job is simply to lock people up. I do not see it that way. If it is possible to regenerate an area socially and economically then you can only do that on the back of a safe environment. If a businessman comes into an area like Glasgow's East End and has to quit after six months because he has been savaged by vandalism and crime, then you inherit a whole range of social problems and other criminal problems. In these circumstances I see the police role as supporting the regenerative process.' Mr Robertson made no claim to original thinking with such an analysis – it was all down to David McNee. It was McNee who embraced the views of the late Geoff Shaw – a man who ministered to Glasgow's deprived and went on to a top role in local politics – that Strathclyde Police was part of the social support mechanism in the region. This philosophy goes on to this day, but at the time it was novel.

In the annals of policing in the West of Scotland, two names tower over all others – McNee and Sillitoe. How 'the Captain' acquired his nickname is self-evident, but there is more controversy over how McNee became 'the Hammer'. However, although there are different versions around, the definitive account comes from David Scott, formerly of the *Sunday Standard* and STV and, of course, the Free Paddy Meehan campaign. David got rather annoyed in March 1982 when Sir David retired as commissioner of the Met. At that time there was – according to the *Standard* – a lot of 'claptrap' in the papers about how the nickname came about. David Scott said: 'The nickname was first used in 1968 when I was a reporter for the old *Daily Express*. I wrote a background story about a notorious Glasgow crook and a city lawyer who were jailed for conspiracy.

'It was alleged that they had tried to persuade others to give false evidence at the murder trial of a man accused of killing Babs Rooney of Govan over moneylending territories. McNee was the man who led the investigation.

'A small piece I had written about him had the headline "The Hammer of the Neds" put on it.' The name stuck.

Certainly, David McNee was instrumental in curbing the 'Tallymen' racket on Clydeside at the time. Tallymen were unofficial moneylenders who demanded extortionate rates of interest on their loans and dealt violently with those who could not meet the payments. It is sad to report that despite the success against them in the '60s and '70s, the archives testify that illegal moneylending went back through the roof in the late '80s and '90s and was once again a disfiguring scar on the face of society in the area.

One writer in the *Evening Times* felt that the Hammer nickname was something of a misnomer because the chief was basically a gentle man who enjoyed family life and music and had a deeply religious background. But David McNee did not object to the accolade when it came to dealing with criminals. 'If people want to call me the Hammer when I am dealing with lawbreakers I have no objection whatsoever,' he said. 'My job is to maintain law and order and *that's* what I have always and will always try to do during my career, wherever I am.'

Another similarity between Sillitoe and McNee was the speed with which they rose up through the ranks to the top job. Sillitoe was 43 when appointed in 1931, while McNee was 45 when promoted in 1971. Bailie James Anderson, a well-kent face in Glasgow local politics over many years, was convener of the police committee at the time, and told the Press: 'Mr McNee has already had a brilliant career in Glasgow. I think he has real qualities of leadership in every respect. I think he is dynamic and he will follow a long line of excellent chief constables in the city.' In these days of huge salaries, even in public service, it is fascinating to read that the salary for the post was £6798 rising to £7674. Sir David had been educated at Woodside Senior Secondary and joined the navy in 1943, serving in the lower deck and taking part in the D-Day landings. On leaving the services in 1946 he joined the police as a constable working in Partick and Anderston. Five years later he was a detective constable in the Marine division and by 1964 he was a detective inspector in the Flying Squad. A couple of years later he moved to the Special Branch as second-in-command. By any standards it was a spectacular rise to the top.

As a hint of what was to come he continued his successful career by being the first Glasgow officer to take a higher command course at Bramshill Police College in England, clearly a man identified as a high achiever with great potential. Back in Scotland he became deputy chief constable of Dunbartonshire. Always a man with high Christian values, the stories of his elevation to the top job in Glasgow noted that he was an elder in the city-centre St George's Tron, where he was closely associated with the famous minister Tom Allan – who made a great mark on religious life in the city, including some much admired journalism, before dying tragically young. The connection with Tom Allan – who was chairman of Billy Graham's 1955 crusade to Glasgow – led to a continuing involvement with the American evangelist. Indeed, Sir David became chairman of the national executive committee of Billy Graham's 1991 Mission to Scotland.

Graham was an inspiration and major influence on McNee. He recalls the Kelvin Hall crusade: 'I can remember night after night hearing the words ringing out – "the Bible says . . . God says". It wasn't what Billy Graham says. I met him many times over that six weeks and found him a wonderful ambassador for Christ and very humble. There was nothing nasty or arrogant about him.'

In the interview about his Graham connection, Sir David went on to recall a crime that has stuck in his mind after all the years of dealing with horrific crimes of all sorts, from gangsterism to international terrorism. It happened to him one New Year's morning when he was working as a young detective. 'A baby had been overlain in bed by drunken parents and suffocated. Looking at this little corpse, who had no way of fending for himself, and these two drunken layabouts, if you will excuse the description, I questioned their right almost to have children.' He is on record as saying that one of the problems of modern society is that parents don't spell out to their children the difference between right and wrong. Right and wrong – aspects of life dealt with by the Hammer year after year in a remarkable police career. However successful he was in Scotland, with saturation policing in problem areas and mobile support units, and in his fight against moneylenders, he went off in 1977 to become Chief of the Met in London and officially Britain's super cop. His last Chief Constable's report in Scotland highlighted a rise in murders, mostly 'domestics' involving drink, and the fact that the police need more resources to fight crime in the area.

In London he faced turbulent years: race riots, IRA terrorism, the Iranian Embassy siege, and the discovery of Michael Fagan in the Queen's bedroom. It almost seemed that there was a new controversy every day – some of it fuelled, it has to be said, by the statements of a straight-talking Scot. The Buckingham Palace incident – and he admitted it was the lowest point in his career – led to calls for his resignation which he resisted. But in 1982 he decided that enough was enough. He was angry and deeply wounded by the calls for his head and it was reported that he argued in private that responsibility for the palace break-in and the discovery of homosexual indiscretions by the Queen's bodyguard was the responsibility of subordinates. On fresh accusations of corruption in the London force he pointed out that he had fought police criminality resolutely.

The then head of the Police Federation, Tony Judge, said: 'Sir David didn't have the luck. It could have been any commissioner at the top – there was nothing he could do about it.

'He has done a good job in difficult circumstances. His reign was overshadowed by Operation Countryman's investigations into corruption and the rumours surrounding it. He also had to deal with the Brixton riots and the growing problem of policing the inner city.

'On the other hand he conducted successful operations against major criminals and terrorism and he encouraged local commanders to get to know the public more. The force has become less remote under his leadership.' The men who followed him have found without exception that leading the Met is a fearsome task. The London *Times* summed up his departure in these words: 'His legacy is a fine one . . . all in all it is not a bad record for Commissioner McNee to take home with him to Glasgow – no mean man returning to no mean city.'

The old 'Captain' Percy Sillitoe, so eager to use new technology, would have had some sympathy for his successors. The archives hold a story of a chief constable who stated that 'a helicopter was a number one priority' for the force. He added: 'We can use a helicopter for many purposes. In a modern police force like Strathclyde I recommend this in the strongest possible terms.' The obvious advantage is that 'in an emergency, specialist officers could be moved to the remoter parts of the region'. The top cop so keen on a private airforce for the men in blue was Sir David NcNee, showing early eagerness to use the latest methods. But it was 14 years later before one of his successors, Andrew Sloan, got the OK to hire a chopper. David McNee was, as often, ahead of his time. But before Strathclyde got round to the eye in the sky – now a familiar sight – the Met in London, the Thames Valley force, Devon and Cornwall and the West Midlands had taken to the air.

The length of service of a Strathclyde police chief varies. The legendary 'Hammer', for example, only served two years before going south. Sir Andrew Sloan left after five years which included some controversial spats with the council, usually over funding. But his final months in the post were marked with discussion over the ideal time for the top man to stay in the job. The Sloan verdict was that 'five years is probably about right. I do not think that a man can work longer at that level without becoming stale, and I believe we have been lucky in the men we have had since Strathclyde came into being'.

There is an old saying that when policemen start to look younger you are growing older. But in the early '90s they began to look smaller when height restrictions on joining, which varied from force to force, were revised. Andrew Sloan had suffered from this in his early career when he was rejected as too small by the City of Glasgow Police, and moved to Yorkshire where he was accepted. When he returned to Glasgow as top cop it was a 'non-operational' regional council appointment and he did not need to meet any height requirement. Andrew Sloan was top cop during the Glasgow Garden Festival in 1988. This massive event on the south bank of the Clyde drew thousands to the city, many of them tourists. There was considerable potential for crime that summer. But it was a great success for the police, and something of a tribute to the people of Glasgow, that during its five-month run there were only 211 minor offences reported. The festival saw Glasgow on its best behaviour.

Every chief constable has his pet projects. Leslie Sharp's years at the helm in Strathclyde had a number of major initiatives. One was Operation Blade. Glasgow's gangsters and neds seemed to have had, over the years, a penchant for knives and razors as weapons of choice. And many a pub in insalubrious areas carried the nickname 'Stab In'. In 1993 Leslie Sharp moved against the knifemen. There was a stop-and-search blitz by police throughout the region and a month-long amnesty for handing in dangerous weapons – Bin the Knife, Save a Life. In the first four days of stop-and-search 1269 suspects were inspected. Forty-two people were arrested and charged with being in possession of an offensive weapon, 28 of which were knives. The haul included a Samurai sword and a machete, proof indeed that the underworld was still something of a jungle! The haul also produced survival knives and kitchen knives.

This campaign was in response to appalling crime figures in 1991 and 1992, when crime rose by 9 per cent. Armed robberies rose dramatically and there was a rise in murders. Almost 3000 attacks on policemen involved weapons. Glasgow's East End was still a major problem, with the area flooded with police – to the detriment of other parts of the city – in order to break the 'wall of silence' caused by fear of feuding drug-dealers. Same old story. And at this stage there was major concern that the police were undermanned, with non-payment of Poll Tax causing cuts in the police budget. But initiatives like Operation Blade – and Operation Eagle, an anti-drugs campaign – were a huge success. Six thousand people were arrested in Operation Eagle and more than 30,000 children given anti-drugs awareness talks in an effort to stamp out the drugs trade. Lack of manpower was perhaps a factor in Leslie Sharp's championing of closed-circuit TV. City Watch was costing around £250,000 a year, but in 1995, as Chief Constable Sharp was about to retire, it was credited with cutting crime and making the city centre, in particular, safer. Leslie Sharp created a Code of

Conduct for CCTV designed to meet civil liberties groups' misgivings.

John Orr, the policeman who followed Leslie Sharp as head of Strathclyde at the beginning of 1996, had a successful run at this toughest of jobs. So much so that he was asked to extend his five-year contract to the maximum of seven years. But he only agreed to stay an extra six months. There was no mystery about cutting the period, just an admission of how hard it can be to be chief constable of Strathclyde. 'It's like 24 hours a day sometimes. You cannot do this job any other way.' One of the factors in his decision to leave was the dawning realisation that he had virtually no private life and that he was spending large periods of time in the flat above the police HQ in Pitt Street in the city centre. Like his successor Willie Rae, Sir John was heavily involved in the Lockerbie tragedy. As joint head of the Strathclyde CID at the time he was drafted in as senior investigating officer into the murder of 270 men, women and children on that fateful night. As a result he has spent much time lecturing on disaster planning, administration and investigation of major incidents.

But John Orr has also been deeply involved in crime at street level. He is a great believer in robust, high-visibility, interventionist policing involving searching large numbers of people for weapons and hammering the drug-dealers. But a constant thread in his interviews is similar to that of his predecessors – lack of funding. 'We have, I believe, not been treated well for the size of the force.' Nonetheless he has presided over many initiatives. His Spotlight campaign – with large groups of highly visible policemen in yellow jackets descending on pubs and other places to show that the forces of law and order were on the job – led to a national campaign, Safer Scotland. His Know the Score initiative saw millions of pounds in drugs seized. As he left office to devote some quality time to the job of chairman of Kilmarnock Football Club – a love since he was a boy – he was able to say, 'Things are getting better'. In his final report he could point to a drop in most categories of crime.

Interesting that this tale of crime in Glasgow, and the war against it down the years, has featured the ravages of gangsterism and violence in particular areas, something of an anathema to John Orr. As he left office he told the *Evening Times* that the whole of society needs to help fight crime. And that there are no 'no go' areas in Glasgow or anywhere in Strathclyde. 'I won't stand for it,' he said.

The recent spate of street whackings and yet another battle for control of the remaining drugs scene notwithstanding, there is no denying that after all these years things are getting better – as fair a verdict as you will get in the continuing fight between good and evil in a modern city.

INDEX